WIN AT BACKGAMMON

BY

MILLARD HOPPER

DOVER PUBLICATIONS, INC.
NEW YORK

This Dover edition, first published in 1972, is an unabridged and unaltered republication of the work originally published in 1941 by A. S. Barnes and Company, Inc., under the title *Backgammon*.

International Standard Book Number: 0-486-22894-0
Library of Congress Catalog Card Number: 72-86224

Manufactured in the United States of America
Dover Publications, Inc.
180 Varick Street
New York, N.Y. 10014

DEDICATED TO:

MY AFFECTIONATE DAUGHTER, JANICE,

MAY SHE WIN ALL OF LIFE'S GAMES.

PREFACE

It has long been my desire to present to the public a simple yet revealing textbook on the playing of Backgammon.

Having completed a book of checkers for the A. S. Barnes Indoor Games Library, it was by a happy combination of circumstances that I was offered the assignment to cover this fascinating and exciting pastime.

Here, I thought, is my long sought opportunity to finally present a book that will keep in mind the learner's viewpoint so that no one will have even the slightest difficulty in mastering the game.

Many learners undertaking a study of this game have been discouraged at the very outset by the confusing references to "Inner and Outer Tables" and other technical terms which has constituted a fault in many otherwise excellent manuals on the game. My constant aim has been to avoid this fault by outlining in simple language the general methods of play. This has been accomplished by introducing a simple presentation of the manner of play, so that the plays can be shown at a glance.

Backgammon, while holding a wealth of strategy and

skill does not require the exacting concentration of chess and checkers. While luck plays a great part in the results of the game where players are equally matched, still, a skillful player when paired against a haphazard one, will far excel his inexperienced adversary.

The present volume has been prepared to meet the needs of those students who require a comprehensive yet simplified manual on the game. Special thanks must be given to my esteemed friend, Dr. Joseph Franklin Montague for the constructive assistance extended me in the preparation of the work.

CONTENTS

CHAPTER 1

HOW OLD IS BACKGAMMON?

Games of skill and intriguing pastimes have captured the imagination of the human race since the world began.

Life, with its wars, worries, and disappointments, has always sought a haven of refuge in the realm of mental diversions.

To play an absorbing game is one of the surest ways of taking tired minds off the monotony of daily routine.

Among the age old favorites of home games that will never die is the entertaining pastime of Backgammon. Its endless diversity of play and amusement will fully compensate all who undertake its study. Young and old alike will find it a fascinating pastime to sharpen their wits and develop logical thinking, foresight, and alertness; faculties well placed for the struggles of everyday life.

The origin of Backgammon is lost in antiquity. It has been played for hundreds of years in almost every country in the world. The Romans referred to it as "Scripta Dodecim"; the French as "Tric Trac," and the early English knew it as "Tables."

In its mode of play in the 13th Century, three dice were used for the throws and the pieces were all started from the adversary's table.

Its latest modifications and the novel introduction of "Doubling" and "Chouette" have added considerable interest and zest to the game: "Doubling" by accelerating its pace and increasing its scoring, and "Chouette," by allowing several players to take part in the game.

The fun of Backgammon is in its constantly changing advantages and startling surprises that occur frequently during the game. Even when your opponent has a seemingly winning advantage over you, one may change to the "Back Game" and often score a brilliant victory.

Today, in the leading clubs, Backgammon is fast supplanting Bridge, and while anyone can learn the game, still to play it skillfully and have a true appreciation of it, requires a knowledge of definite strategies of play.

While the element of luck enters into the game in a big way, and while skill cannot always triumph over chance, yet a constant application of skill, will, with rare exceptions, outgeneral the haphazard plays of the novice.

CHAPTER 2

HOW IS THE GAME PLAYED?

Backgammon is played by two persons upon a board designed with twenty-four points of alternate colors.

Each player is provided with a set of dice, a dice box, and fifteen men or checkers, one set of men generally being Black and the other White.

The colors of the men or checkers varies with the different grades of sets, but Black and White, or Red and White are the most customary. Actually you can play with men of any color provided your pieces are of a contrasting color from your opponents.

The following diagram shows the Backgammon Board before the pieces have been set up for Play.

The Board is divided into four sections or "tables" each player having an "outer" and "home" table facing him, each table containing six points.

The men are moved along the points on the far side of the board, then across the board until they reach their Home tables, from which they are moved off the board. The player first bearing all his men is declared the winner.

Direction of Moving

The men are moved from point to point according to the throws of the dice.

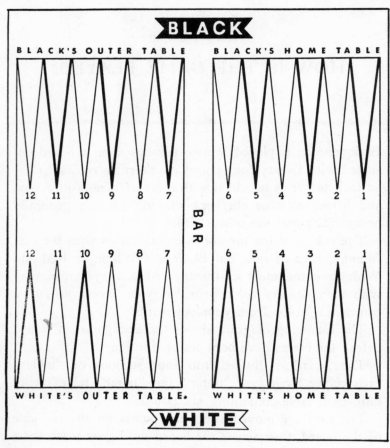

DIAGRAM I

The Backgammon Board

The points having heavy outlines are generally of different color on the actual board but as the alternate colors of the points does not enter into the playing of the game we have simply designated them by a light and dark outline.

Diagram 2 shows the movement of the pieces. The points are numbered in the Diagrams to facilitate the explanation of the moves, although the regular playing board carries no numbers or references to tables.

The division in the center of the board is known as the Bar.

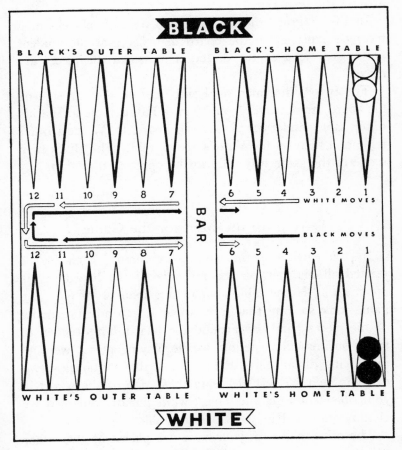

DIAGRAM 2

The Direction of the Moves

The White pieces move in the direction of the white arrows until they reach their home table. The Black's as shown by the Black arrows, move in the opposite direction so that the players men pass each other as they travel around the board.

In the diagram shown, only two of each players men have been placed on the board in order that the student get a clear idea of the direction in which the pieces are moved.

The two White men on Point one, on the far side of the board, must travel from Black's Home table to Black's outer table, and then across the board to White's outer table and then on to White's Home table. The Black men move in the same way only in the opposite direction.

Setting up the Men for the Game

In the earliest forms of Backgammon, each player started all his men on the far side of the board in his opponent's "Home table" but in this manner of play, the game took so long that it was decided to advance many of the pieces part way around the board. This tended to bring on immediate action, as the playing pieces were all in striking distance of each other. In this set-up only two of your men are left at the farthest side of the board in your opponent's "Home table," while five of your men are already stationed in your "Home table."

The other eight of your men are placed at two other points in what is known as the "Outer Tables."

The following diagram shows the regular set-up of the White men for the start of the game.

The position should be set up on the Backgammon Board.

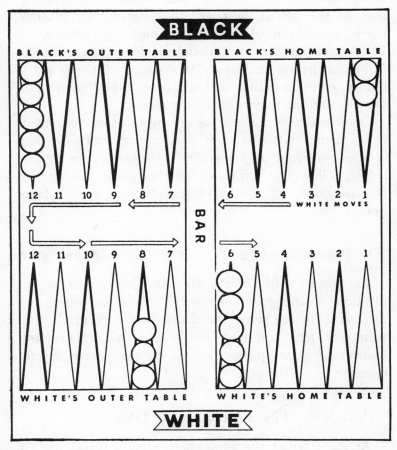

DIAGRAM 3

The White Men Set-Up for Play

The student will notice how the White pieces are distributed at four different points on the road to the Home table. White has two men on the last point in Black's Home table which must travel the farthest to reach home. White, also, has five men in Black's Outer table ready to cross to his side of the board to continue their journey home, and White also has three men just outside his Home table and five men already in his Home table.

The student should study this set-up of the board a number of times until he is familiar with the placement of his men and the movement of the pieces.

Once you have learned the arrangement of your men, it is a simple matter to set up the opponent's men *for they occupy corresponding points directly opposite your men.*

The following diagram shows the board set up ready for the game, with both White and Black men in position.

The Board Set up for Play at the Start of the Game

The reader will observe how the Black men are in identical positions opposite the White's. In setting up the board for the game, the easiest way is to first set up your own men and then simply place a corresponding number of your opponent's men on the points directly opposite.

The Throws of the Dice

At the start of the game, both players throw *one* of the dice and the highest wins. If they throw the same number, they must throw again, the player getting the

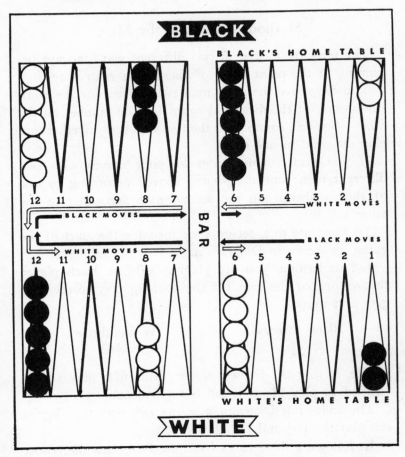

DIAGRAM 4

highest number being entitled to the first play, and plays his own and his opponent's throw for his first move.

After the first throw, the players use both dice and take turns with the throws until the game is completed.

Method of Moving the Men

The men are moved in two different ways, always beginning at the point next to where your man is resting.

You can move the same man twice; once for the number on one of the dice, and again for the number on the other—but you cannot add the two numbers together and play the total in one move.

If you prefer, you can make your moves with two different men; one man being moved according to one of the numbers, and the second man according to the other number.

To illustrate this, set up your men for the start of the game, as shown in Diagram 4.

Let us assume you are playing Whites. Each player throws one of the dice for the opening play to see who gets first move.

Black throws	White throws
[5]	[6]

White, having the highest throw, wins first play and is entitled to play his [6] and his opponent's [5].

The following Diagram 5 shows one way that White can play the [6] and [5] throw.

In following these plays from the Diagrams the reader should make the actual plays on his Backgammon board. This enables you to register the mechanics of the plays in your mind and gives an opportunity to judge the distances between the various points without having to count each point as you make your move. As the Diagram shows a six play will take you from one table into another.

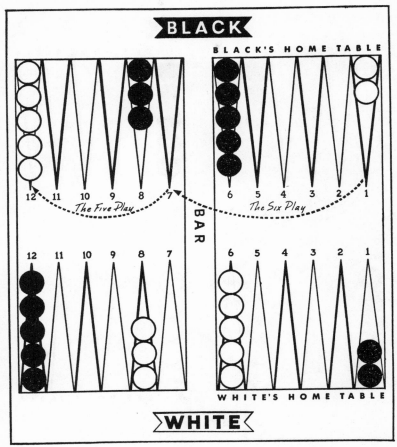

DIAGRAM 5

White Playing a [6] and [5]

White plays his [6] and [5] by moving one of his men from Black's 1 point to Black's 7 point for the [6] and he then plays the [5] by moving the same man from point 7 over five more points to Black's 12 point.

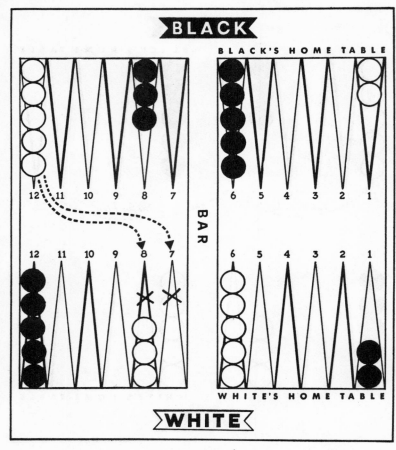

DIAGRAM 6

Now suppose the White decided to play the [6] and [5] throw of the dice another way. See Diagram 6.

White can play his [6] and [5] throw by playing two men from Black's 12 point, as shown by the dotted lines.

The [6] and [5] played this way leaves three men on point 12 and adds one man to White's 7 point and one man to his 8 point, as shown by the crosses on these points.

White might also have played the [6] and [5] by moving one man from Black's 12 point to White's 7 point for the [6], and then playing the same man five points forward to his own 2 point for the [5]. This, however, would leave the single man on White's 2 point in a dangerous position where it might easily be hit on the next play by one of your opponent's men on point 1 in your Home table.

You must bear in mind that your opponent's Black men are coming towards you; also that a single man on any point is subject to being hit and sent back to start over.

Still another way that White may have played his [6] or [5] throw is shown on diagram 7.

Here, White plays his [6] and [5] by moving two men from point 8. One man to point 2 for the [6] and one man to point 3 for the [5]. This is an extremely poor play, for it leaves single men on points 3 and 2, which offer a swell target for Black's men on Point 1 which are moving towards White, and which can hit these men with a throw of [2] and [1].

Blocked Points

A point that has two or more men on it is said to be "Blocked" and an opponent cannot play a man on that point; he can, however, move a man past a blocked point, provided the number being played would bring the man past that point.

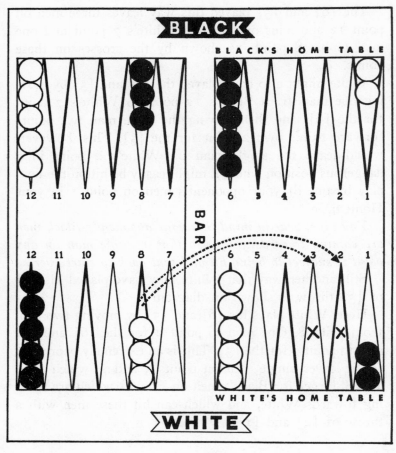

DIAGRAM 7

As a Blocked point impedes the advance of your opponent's men, it is a great advantage to secure as many blocked points as possible. An illustration of this is as follows: White gets an opening throw on the dice of a [3] and [1] and plays it to secure another Blocked point. Diagram 8 pictures the play completed.

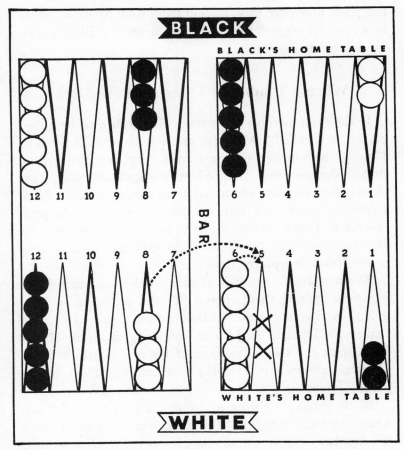

DIAGRAM 8

Here White has played his [3] and [1] by moving one
man from his 8 point to his 5 point, and another man
from his 6 point to his 5 point. This leaves point 5
Blocked to your opponent as it holds more than one man.
If White can manage to move two men to his 7 point or

bar point at a later play, he will have four Blocked Points in a row, which will be a difficult barrier for Black's men on point 1 to hurdle.

When a Double Is Thrown on the Dice

If the same number is thrown with both dice by either player, it is called "Doublets" and the player is entitled to Double the number of his moves. For instance: if he throws double sixes, [6] [6] he is entitled to play [two sixes], and then an additional [two sixes] in any of the following ways: All four (6 plays) can be made with one man, if he has open points to land on, or the play can be made by two, three, or four different men in any combination the player desires.

As an example, we will assume White has started the game by making the [3] and [1] throw shown in Diagram 8 and your opponent Black, on his throw of the dice makes a [Double Six]. The following diagram shows how Black can take advantage of his throw, which being Doublets allows him to make four moves of six points each.

Black, getting a throw of [double sixes] takes full advantage of the fact that "Doublets" entitles him to twice the number of moves, and plays his two furthermost men from White's 1 point to White's 7 point for the first [two sixes], and then plays two more men from White's 12 point to his own 7 point for the remaining [two sixes]. This gives Black a strong advantage for it brings four of his men quite a distance home; also it enables him to block the two points next to the Bar which are known as Bar points, and are valuable points to occupy. As the

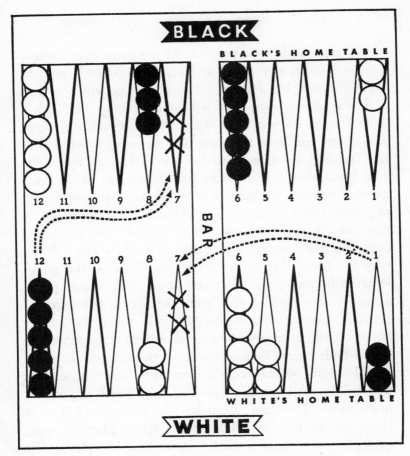

DIAGRAM 9

diagram also shows, Black now has three consecutive
points blocked on his side, namely points 6, 7, or bar
point and 8. A blockade of this kind should be retained
as long as possible, as it hinders the release of the two
White men on point 1.

Blots

Any time during the progress of the game that a single man is left on any point, it is called a "Blot," and, as explained, may be "Hit" by either player, provided he gets a throw of the dice that will land him on that point. This hazard of leaving a Blot which is often compulsory when you have no other play to make is what adds the fun and excitement to the game. It also opens the way for a wealth of strategy for ofttimes as in the Back game, Blots are left purposely as "decoys" to tempt your opponent into hitting same. A "blot" hit by your opponent can set you back several throws of the dice and often cost you the loss of the game. The following shows why the Blot is often the Knockout Blow of the game. When a player hits a "Blot" or single man on any point, he moves his man to that point, removing the captured man and placing it upon the "Bar" in the center of the board. This man must be reentered in the opponents Home table before he can play any other moves. This can only be done by throwing a number which entitles him to enter the man on an unoccupied point in his opponent's home table. The man is entered the same as if it were being played from a point off the table. The following examples show how a Blot is left; how the player hits same, and how the piece is reentered in the opponent's home table.

The student should make the moves on his Backgammon board to better visualize the plays.

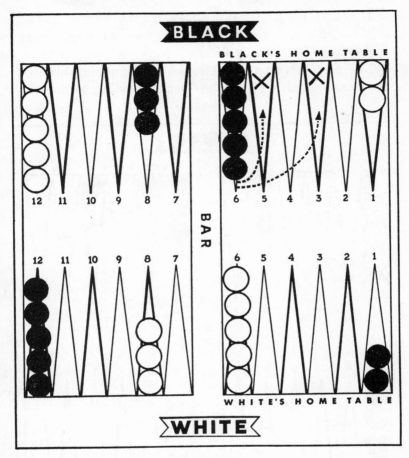

DIAGRAM 10

In the above diagram, Black has won the opening throw of the dice for a [3] and [1].

Black plays his [3] and [1] in the weakest possible way by leaving two single men on Blots on Points 3 and 5 in his Home table, where they are subject to being hit by White's two men on Point 1.

It is now White's turn to throw the dice and he throws a "Doublet" or [double twos]. Diagram 11 shows what happens to Black's two "Blots."

White plays his first [double two's] by moving his two men from Black's 1 point to Black's 3 point, hitting the

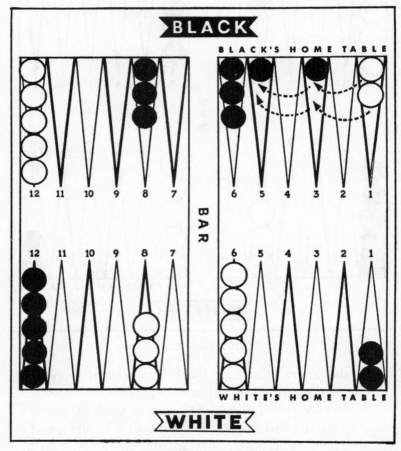

DIAGRAM 11

single man or Blot on that point and sending the Black man to the Bar to be restarted. He then advances the same two men for the additional [double two's] to point 5 and hits the second Black Blot on that point. This Black man is also removed and sent to the Bar. Diagram 12 shows the situation after White has completed his plays.

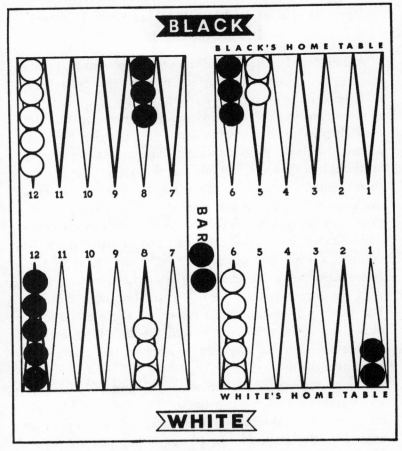

DIAGRAM 12

Black's two single men that were hit are now placed on the Bar and must be re-entered in White's Home table, and must be moved all around the board again to reach their home table. White's two men have advanced to Black's 5 point and have that point blocked.

Restarting a Man After He Has Been Hit and Placed on the Bar

A man that has been "hit" by your opponent and placed on the Bar must be restarted in the *opponent's Home table* before the player can move any other man. The man is re-entered by the throw of the dice, provided the numbers thrown enable him to land on an open point not already blocked by his opponent. The men are re-entered as though they are being played on to the board, a [1] throw entitles a man to enter on the 1 point a [2] on the 2 point, a [3] on the 3 point, and so on up to [6], each man being entered for the exact numbers thrown.

For example, in diagram 12, just shown, Black has two men on the Bar which must be re-entered *in White's Home table* before he can move any other men.

If his throw enables him to enter one man from the Bar he can do so but the number on the die cannot be moved until the other man from the Bar is entered. If neither man on the Bar can be entered the player loses his entire throw.

Let us assume Black throws a [1] and [6]. The [1] will enable him to re-enter one of his men from the Bar on point 1 in White's Home table, but he cannot re-enter his other man for the [6] *as White has the 6 point blocked*. Diagram 13 shows the situation.

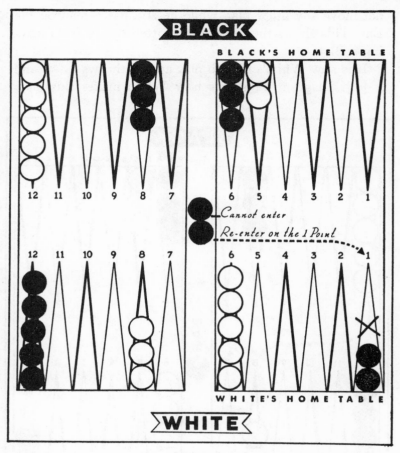

DIAGRAM 13

Black with two men on the Bar has thrown a [1] and
[6]. He re-enters one man from the Bar on Point 1 in
White's Home table, but cannot enter for the [6] as the
6 point contains more than two of White's men and is
Blocked. Black, therefore, loses his [6]throw as he can-

not move any other man while he still has a man on the Bar. This shows the penalty that often comes from leaving a Blot.

It is now White's turn to play and he throws a [5] and a [1]. Diagram 14 shows how White makes this play.

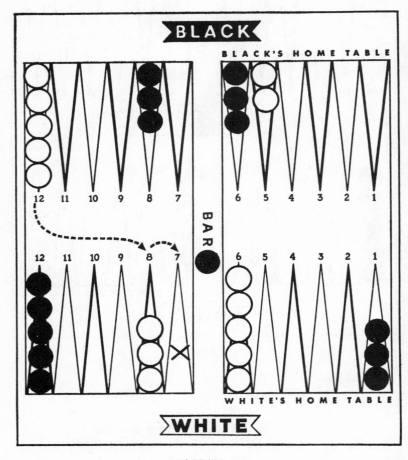

DIAGRAM 14

White's throw of a [5] and [1] happened to be a poor one, for it forces him to leave a single man or "Blot" on some point. As the Diagram shows, he plays one man from Black's 12 point to his own 8 point for the [5], and for the [1] advances the same man to his 7 point. This leaves a "Blot" on White's 7 point, which he hopes to cover on his next play.

In this instance White was in a position where he was compelled to leave a Blot no matter how he played but there are many players who will leave a Blot on the Bar point without being compelled to, banking on the chance that his opponent will not be able to hit the man, in which case he may be able to cover his Blot on the next play and secure that valuable point. However as shown later the risk far exceeds the advantage that might be gained.

It is now Black's play and he throws a [6] and a [1]. This time, Black gets the lucky break for, by playing the [1] first, he re-enters his man from the Bar on White's 1 point, and then is entitled to play the [6] which he does by moving the same man six points forward to White's 7 or bar point, where he hits White's "Blot" on that point and sends White's man to the Bar. The Diagram illustrates the play.

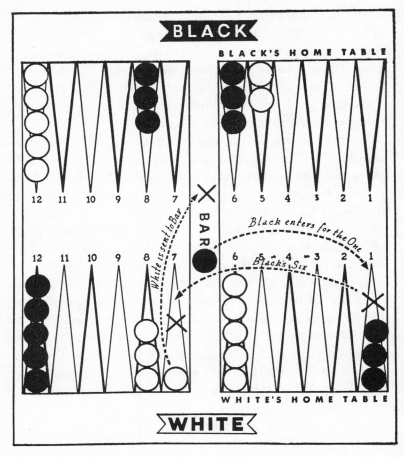

DIAGRAM 15

Black, throwing a [6] and [1] re-enters his man from the Bar on White's one point for the [1] and then plays the [6] by moving the same man to White's 7 or bar point, hitting White's blot on that point and sending it to the Bar; the dotted lines indicate the plays and the X marks the spot where the pieces land.

Bearing Off the Men at the Close of the Game

When a player has succeeded in moving all of his men around the board to his home table, he can begin to take them off the board. This is called "bearing" the men.

For every number thrown, a man is removed from the corresponding point. Thus, if you have all your men in your Home table and you throw a [6] and [3] you can remove a man from the 6 and the 3 point. If you throw a [5] and [4], you can remove men from your 5 and 4 points, and so on for each corresponding number thrown. The following diagram explains this and shows the exact mechanics of bearing your men at the close of the game. There is considerable strategy involved in this final stage of play and is treated at more length later in this book. Right now the student should learn the method of removing the men and this is shown in detail in the following diagrams.

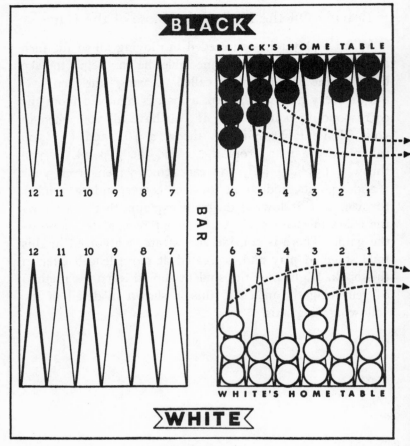

DIAGRAM 16

White throws a [6] and [3] and removes a man from his 6 point and another from his 3 point.

Black throws a [5] and [4] and is entitled to remove men from his 5 and 4 point.

A doublet or double throw, of course, permits a player to remove double the number of men for instance:

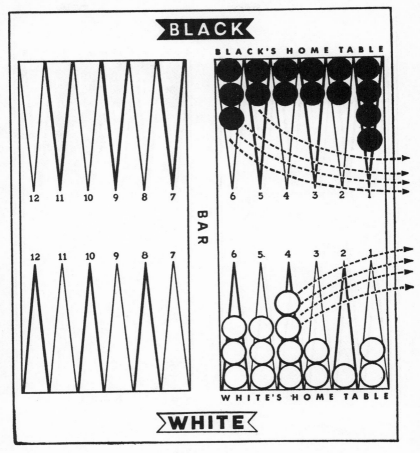

DIAGRAM 17

Here, White has thrown a [Double 4] and removes four men from his 4 point.

Black has thrown [Double Sixes] and only having 3 men on his 6 point is entitled to remove the three men from his 6 point and one man from his next highest point.

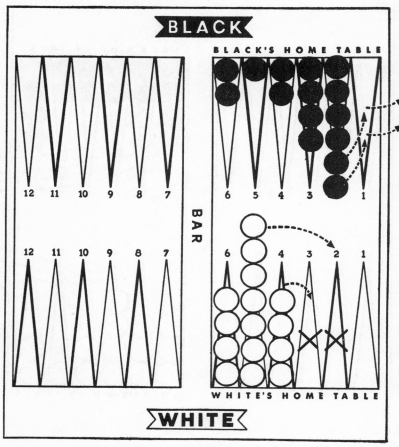

DIAGRAM 18

Should you play a [6] and [5] and have previously removed all your men from these points, you are entitled to remove two men from the next highest occupied points.

If low numbers are thrown and you have no man on the corresponding points, but have men on higher numbered points, you must play up the men from the higher points as shown in Diagram 18.

Here, White throws a [3] and a [1]; he has no men on the 3 or 1 points, so must move up some of his men from the higher to the lower points. He can move one or two men from any occupied point for the plays. In the Diagram, he moves a man from the 5 to the 2 point for the [3] and a man from the 4 to the 3 for the [1].

Now let us suppose it's Black's throw in the same diagram and he throws double [1's]. Having no men on his 1 point he must play up four of his men from his higher points or play up two men from his 2 point to his 1 point and then play off the same men from his 1 point. Diagram 18 shows the play on the Board.

The student must remember that "Doublets" or Doubles on the dice always entitle you to play twice the regular throw.

A player always has the choice of playing his men up the board if it is possible and he prefer to do so.

This is a valuable thing to remember when, as the occasion often arises, your opponent has a man still left in your home table or a man on the Bar which can still hit a blot or single man if you should leave it on a point.

The following example illustrates this important strategy of the end game.

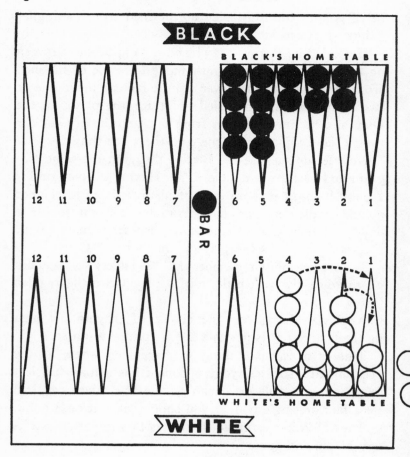

DIAGRAM 19

In this setting, White has already borne two men from the board and has a winning advantage. He throws a [3] and [1] and if he were to play it by removing a man from the 3 point and 1 point, he would leave blots on both these points which may be hit by the Black man, who is going to re-enter in White's Home table. If one of these White "Blots" were hit and had to start over, he would have a hard time of it for Black has five blocked points in his Home table.

White, therefore, plays safe for his [3] and [1] throw and moves his men up instead of bearing them. He moves a man from the 4 point to the 1 point for the [3] and a man from the 2 point to the 1 point for the [1]. Diagram 19 shows the play.

Care must always be taken when bearing your men if Black has any men in front of your men in your Home table or upon the Bar.

Scoring

The player who first bears all his men from the Board wins a Single Game.

If a player has borne all his men before his opponent has borne any, the player wins a Double Game or "Gammon."

If the loser has not borne a man, and still has one or more men in his opponent's "Home Table," or upon the Bar, when the winner has borne all his men, the winner is entitled to a Triple Game or "Backgammon."

It is generally the rule that the winner of the first game has the first throw of the dice in the succeeding game, but this is usually agreed upon prior to the beginning of play.

The purpose of counting Gammons and Backgammons as Double and Triple games is to allow the winner to earn a suitable award for winning a decisive victory. By giving a player a chance to double or triple the score, more aggressiveness is added to the game.

There is also a scoring method in vogue in some cities whereby the players play for "points." In this system, the winner scores one point for every man of his opponent's remaining on the board at the end of the game.

If the game ends in a Gammon, the number is doubled and if a Backgammon the total is tripled.

Still another system of scoring used by players is to eliminate the Gammons and Backgammons entirely, and to base the score entirely on "points." In this system, the winner scores one point for every man of his opponent's remaining in his opponent's Home table; two points for every man remaining in his opponent's outer table; three points for every man in the winner's outer table and 4 points for every man remaining in the winner's Home table or upon the Bar.

While this last method of scoring has been accepted by many players, I still prefer to retain the traditional Gammon and Backgammon.

CHAPTER 3

AN ILLUSTRATIVE GAME

Now that our students have a clear understanding of the rudiments of play, we will take him over part of a game. (The student should make the plays on his board and refer to the diagrams.)

After each play it would be well to study the situation carefully, noting the reason why the plays were made. This will register the movements and purpose of the plays and speed up your playing ability.

The players each throw one dice to decide who gets the opening play, and White wins the throw, a [3] and [1], one of the best opening throws in the game.

White winning the [3] and [1] throw, plays it in the best way possible, by blocking the 5 point in· his Home table.

It is now Black's throw and he throws a [1] and [1]. This being a double and the strongest possible opening throw on the dice, enables him to cover his 5 point in his Home table, also his 7 or Bar Point. Diagram 20 shows these plays indicated on the board.

Both players are aiming at securing a row of Blocked Points to block the escape of the opponent's two men in their inner table.

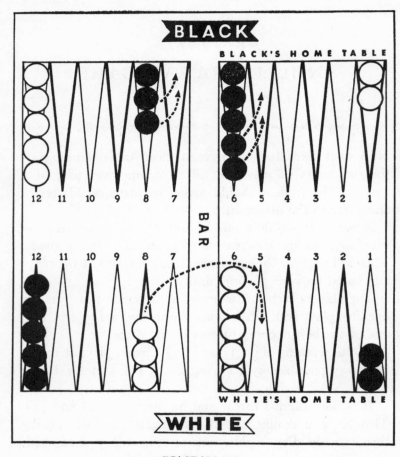

DIAGRAM 20

Black's throw of a Double has left a blot on his 8 point but the chances are very slim that White will get a throw that will enable him to hit this man.

White now throws a [5] and [1] and plays a man from Black's 12 point to his own 8 point for the [5] and continues the same man to his 7 or Bar point for the 1.

This leaves a blot on White's 7 point but if Black fails to hit it on the next play, White has a good chance of covering it (This is always a risky play, for Black has an even chance of making a 6 and hitting this blot.)

Black now throws a [3] and [2], and immediately moves a man from White's 12 point to his own 8 point. This covers the single man or "Blot" on this point and likewise gives him 4 consecutive blocked points. The following diagram shows the situation after these plays have been made.

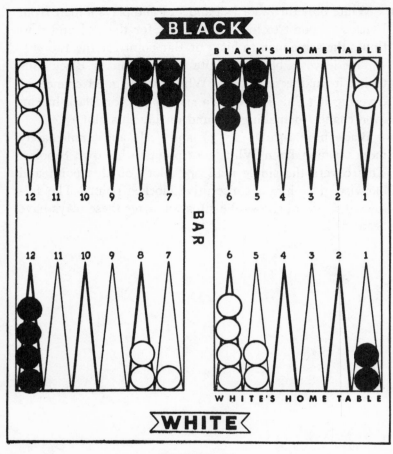

DIAGRAM 21

It is White's play and he throws a [6] and [2]. For the [6] he immediately moves a man from Black's 12 point over to his 7 or bar point to cover the White single man on that point and give him 4 blocked points in a row. For White's [2] he plays another man from Black's 12

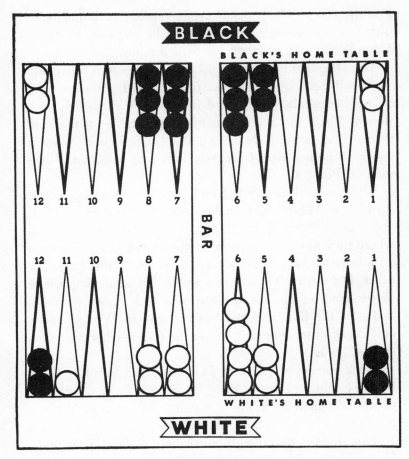

DIAGRAM 22

point to his own 11 point. This leaves a Blot on his 11 point, but the blot is safe here, for Black cannot hurdle your 4 Blocked Points with any throw and strike this man.

It is now Black's play and he throws a [6] and [5].

For the [6] he plays a man from White's 12 point to his own 7 or bar point, and for the [5] he plays another man from White's 12 point to his own 8 point.

The Diagram herewith shows the game up to this point.

As will be seen, Black has four blocked points, several of which contain 3 men, and is in a very favorable position to Block the 4 point in his Home table on the next throw. Such a blockade known as a "Side Prime" when it covers 6 points would securely bottle up the two White men on Point 1.

White now throws a [3] and [3]. This is an opportune throw for White, and enables him to advance his outposts from Point 1 in Black's Home table to Point 4, where they are in a position to hurdle the Black blockade on a later throw of double fives or sixes. White plays the other [two three's] of his Double by advancing the 2 White men on Black's 12 point over to his own 10 point, and now the tide of battle has changed in White's favor and Black must endeavor to get his two furthermost men started home.

Black throws a [2] and [1]. Now Black boldly plays the [2] and [1] by moving, two men from White's 1 point: one man to White's 3 point, and one to White's 2 point.

This leaves two single men or "blots" in White's Home Table, either of which White can very likely hit on his next throw. The diagram shows the position at this stage of the game.

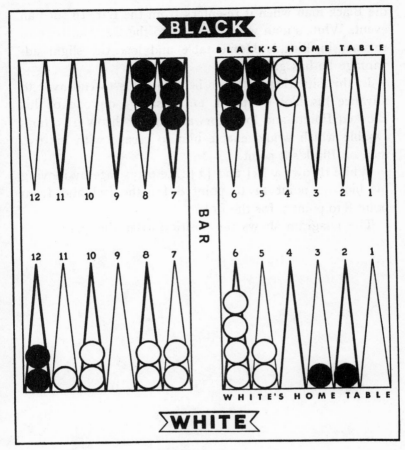

DIAGRAM 23

Now White having a definite lead on Black must be cautious about hitting those two blots that Black left on points 2 and 3. He must remember that if he hits one of the blots and cannot block the point at the same time, his own single man on that point will be liable to be re-hit by the Black man when it re-enters from the Bar. In such an event, White's man would be sent to the Bar and have to re-start in Black's Home table and lose the slight advantage he has gained.

In this situation, White's best policy is to endeavor to advance his blot on point 11 to safety on one of his Blocked Points and look forward to the throw of a high Double which would enable him to escape with his two men on Black's 4 point.

White throws a [3] and [1]. He plays safe by moving his blot on point 11 to point 8 for the [3] and from point 8 to point 7 for the [1].

The Diagram shows the position after this play.

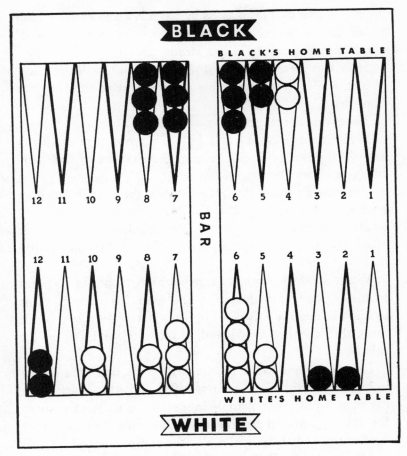

DIAGRAM 24

It is Black's play and he throws a [2] and [5].

He moves a man from White's 12 point to his own 11 point for the [2] and continues the same man from the 11 point to the 6 point in his Home table for the [5].

This was Black's best play as he has advanced another man to his blockade and is in a good position to secure additional Blocked points in his Home table.

If he can secure these and manage to. hit a White Blot, White will have considerable difficulty in re-entering the "hit" man.

The game continues:

White throws a [4] and [1]. This was a poor throw for White, but in Backgammon, the element of luck ofttimes can turn the tide of battle.

White must make the best of a bad throw. He can play a man to hit one of Black's Blots, but that is exactly what Black desires, for it would enable him to come back from the Bar and, in all probability, re-hit the White man.

White's safest play is to move a man from his 10 point to his 6 point, and then play the man from his 6 point to his 5 point. He leaves a blot on his 10 point, but Black must throw either a [6] and [1] or [6] and [2] to hit this blot.

Let us assume, as often happens, that bad luck comes in bunches—and Black throws a [6] and [1]. Black plays his man from point 3 in White's Home table to point 9 for the [6] and then continues the same man to point 10 for the [1], hitting the White man on that point and sending it to the Bar.

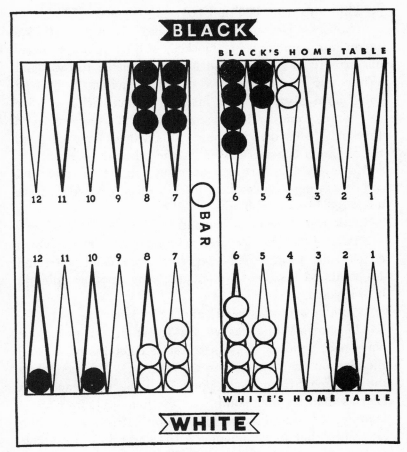

DIAGRAM 25

The diagram shows the situation after these plays.

Now, White is on the defensive and his man on the Bar has to travel a hard road to hurdle the Black blockade on Black's points 5, 6, 7 and 8. Not alone that, but White must cast a [1], [2], [3], or [4] to re-enter this man and continue his plays.

White throws a [6] and [6].

Again, the elements of chance have swung in Black's favor, for point 6 being blocked, White cannot re-enter his man from the Bar and loses a valuable throw. Had White got this double six on the previous throw, he could have advanced both his men from Black's 4 point to the 10 point, and then continued the same two men forward to his own 9 point. This would have changed the situation considerably in White's favor.

However, the fortunes of chance must be met and White casting double sixes loses a play that would have advanced him 24 points.

Black now throws a [6] and [4].

Again, Black has secured a formidable throw which enables him to move his two blots from White's 10 and 12 points to his own 9 point, securing another point in his blockade.

White now throws a [3] and [3].

This time, White has won a fortunate throw and he plays it as follows: He must first re-enter his man from the Bar on the 3 point for the first [3]. He then plays the two men from his 5 point to his 2 point and hits Black's man on that point. For the final [3], he plays a man from his 8 point to his 5 point. This leaves a blot on point 8, but Black must get a [3] and a [5] or [double fours] to strike it, and Black only has three open points to enter on.

Black throws a [2] and [2].

This time Black loses his throw, as White has the 2 point blocked.

White now throws [4] and [2].

Again White takes advantage of this throw to secure another point in his Home table, and plays a man from his 8 to his 4 point, and another from his 6 to his 4 point.

Now Black's worries start to pile up, for if he does not throw a [1] or [3] on the next cast, White may be able to block still another point in the Home table and possibly maroon the Black man on the Bar.

This time, Black throws a [1] and a [2], and re-enters his man on point 1 in White's Home table; then moves it to point 3 for the 2.

Black could have played the 2 by hitting White's blot on point 3 in his own Home table, but that would leave three Black blots subject to almost a certain hit on the next play. By Black advancing his restarted man to point 3, he is in a better position to escape from White's Home table, if White fails to hit the man on the next throw.

The Diagram shows the position at this stage.

White now throws a [6] and [6] and takes advantage of the high double to liberate his two men on point 4 in Black's Home table. He moves these two men to the 10

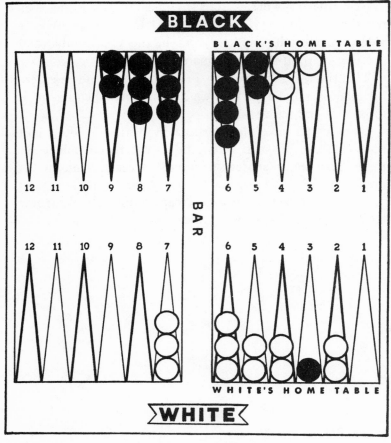

DIAGRAM 26

point and then continues them forward across the table to his 9 point for the other [two sixes].

Now the game can turn in either player's favor if they secure the proper throws. If Black throws a [5] he can escape from White's Home table, whereas, if Black fails to accomplish this and the White checker in Black's Home table manages to make his escape by a throw of [6] and [1], the fortunes would be entirely in White's favor.

As we have pointed out the general tactics of play, we will now introduce the student to the three different types of games and then continue into the more advanced strategies.

In all these plays demonstrated we have assumed that the reader has been sitting at White's side of the board playing the White pieces. From this viewpoint your far-thest White men move from Right to Left, however if you were sitting on Black's side of the board playing the Black pieces, your two furthermost pieces would move from Left to Right. A simple way to see how the board appears when playing the Black men is to set up the pieces for the start of the game and then turn the board around so that Black's Home table is facing you. By studying the set-up of the pieces you will be familiar with both the Black as well as the White side of the game.

CHAPTER 4

THE THREE TYPES OF GAMES

There are three distinct styles or types of play in Backgammon. They are:

1. The Running game.
2. The Blocking game.
3. The Back game.

The selection of which style of game you play depends to a great extent on the dice.

Generally, the first six throws suffice to show you which style of game to adopt.

A player getting several high throws at the start of the game is practically forced to accept a "Running" game.

If the initial throws of the dice enable you to secure a number of Blocked Points, the player has the opportunity of playing a "Blocking" game, which, besides being safest, generally holds the best chances of victory.

The Back game is only adopted as an alternative when your opponent has gained an overwhelming lead in the game. The Back game is really a defensive measure used as a last resort to prevent a defeat. Some writers on Backgammon have added another type of game called the "Position" game, which they classify as a watchful waiting game.

Actually, watchful waiting and caution are a part of every game and carries no specific type of play, like the other games. The variety or style of play, of course, changes from time to time during the game. A player may start with a "Running Game," switch to a "Blocking Game" and finally revert to a "Back Game."

Just when to abandon one game and change to another depends on the situation of the game. To enable the student to gain a clear insight into each of these styles of games, we will treat each separately.

The Running Game

The Running Game is usually adopted when you get several high throws at the very outset of the game and have a definite lead over your opponent. It is the simplest and frequently the most exciting.

Everything is subordinated to full speed ahead and no effort is made to block your opponent. If you can hold the lead with the subsequent throws of the dice, *and avoid being hit,* you should win out in the home table.

However, "hits" are difficult to avoid when a poor throw forces you to leave a vulnerable blot, and you must bear in mind that when a man is hit after it has reached its home table, it must re-enter and cover about 24 points to carry it around the board again.

As Eight is the average throw of the dice, it will take about three average throws to regain your position again.

It is obvious that one or two hits would soon overcome any superiority you might have gained over your opponent by getting a series of high initial throws.

The student will realize by this that the Running Game is rather dangerous, yet with the great advantage of exceptionally large throws at the commencement of the game, it is well worth the risk.

If you are not slowed up by poor throws, the initial advantage offers a good opportunity to win.

If your opponent has retained his two outposts in his home table, which he will undoubtedly do in a game of this kind, care should be taken for the safe arrival of your home-coming men. At this stage, points in the board should be made or blocked and if a blot must be made, try and make it at a point where it will take a combination throw of the two dice to hit it, which would be a point 7 points or more away from the opponent's men.

The main rules to remember on the running game are:

1. Always retreat your outpost first.

2. Avoid hitting blots until your inner table is closed, the points being occupied by your men.

3. After you have passed your opponent, try to play your throws so that each number will carry a man into your home table, or from any one table to another.

The Defense Against a Running Game

The best defense against a Running game is to try and build a blockade somewhere along the points to slow up your opponent's progress.

Ofttimes, if your opponent has adopted a Running game and *is not too far ahead,* you can play a Running game yourself as the dice may favor you in a few throws.

Another counter to the Running Game is a Back game, but this must be adopted just as soon as your opponent has a winning lead over you; otherwise it will not prove effective.

The Blocking Game

The safest and soundest game to adopt is the Blocking Game, and it holds many opportunities for a Gammon or Double Game.

The object, of course, is to block as many points in a row as possible and thus prevent the escape of the opponent's two men in your Home table.

Certain opening throws enable a player to start blocking these obstructive points; for instance, an opening throw of [Double 1] will enable a player to immediately occupy the 5 point in your Home table and your Bar point, which immediately starts an effective barrier to your opponent's two men in your Home table.

An opening throw of [6] and [1] also allows you to secure three consecutive points and an adversary who is alert will lose no time in endeavoring to release his two men from the impending blockade.

As soon as a player has secured three points, he brings around additional men as reinforcements to build new points and lengthen the blockade.

Once you have blocked four or five points, your opponent will find it extremely difficult for his two men to escape and if you are able to block six points in a row termed a ("side prime"), your opponent's two men are completely locked up in your Home table. The highest single number he can throw on the dice is [6] and, as the nearest point he can land on is seven points distant, he is unable to move his two men as long as you can retain your "side prime." This "side prime" is effective at any location on the board, but generally is grouped from the 9 to the 4 point inclusive.

Once you have imprisoned your opponent's men with this type of blockade, you should work your additional men round to join these men and then, finally, work the side prime steadily forward into your Home table.

A "side prime" should not be broken and, when it is compulsory to move it forward, this can be done by first reforming additional points ahead. The following diagram shows exactly how a "side prime" is kept intact, yet moved forward into your Home table.

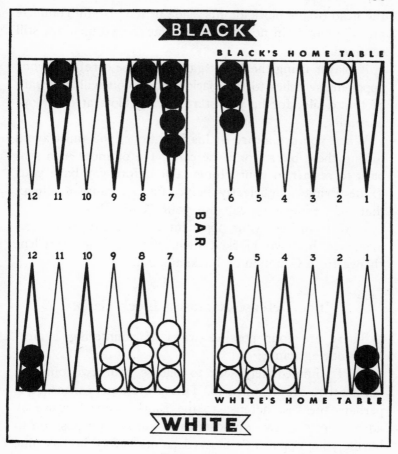

DIAGRAM 27

Here White throws a [6] and [4].

He can shift his "side prime" one step forward by playing a man from his 9 point to his 3 point, and another man from his 7 point to his 3 point. This leaves a blot on point 9, but, as White has reformed a new point at the head of his blockade his "side prime" is still complete and the blot is in no danger, as Black's two men are still confined.

A player using the Block game must be careful if your opponent switches to the Back Game. You will be aware of this easily, for he will start leaving blots at every opportunity.

When you are aware of his intentions, you must avoid hitting these blots, for if he can get 4 or more men sent back to restart in your Home table before you have your "Side Prime" sufficiently home, he can cause a climax that may completely collapse your "Side Prime."

If you can keep your opponent from adding reinforcements to his two blocked men, you have an excellent chance for a Gammon or Backgammon.

The Defense Against a Block Game

There are four possible ways of countering against the Blocking game:

1. To immediately seek to release your two outposts before they are hemmed in. This preventative measure is perhaps the best defense to the Block Game because by advancing your two outposts they will be in a position to hurdle your opponent's blocked points before he has time to lengthen his blockade into a "Side Prime." If your opponent has secured three Blocked points in a row and is bringing around builders, *your outposts must be advanced immediately,* even if you must separate your two men and leave blots. Once these two men have advanced to the front of his blockade, you can use your high throws to hurdle same and effect their escape. If he should hit

your blots at this stage, he will be taking a big risk, for your man may rehit him on entering.

2. Another defense to the Block Game is to retaliate with a counter "Side Prime" on your side of the board, but the relative positions must be nearly equal to fight a Block Game with a Block Game.

3. Still another counter to the Block Game is to build a closed Home Table and depend on possible hits on your opponent's men as he moves his "Side Prime" forward toward your two outposts, however, a "Side Prime" once established is a great advantage to overcome.

4. The other alternative against the Block Game is in switching to a Back Game, but this must be decided upon before your opponent's blockade has spread over the majority of open points in his Home table.

The Back Game

The Back Game is generally the favorite of the beginner who drifts into it naturally by recklessly leaving blots on exposed points. The expert player only resorts to it when his opponent has made a series of favorable opening throws which puts him so far ahead that your position is hopeless.

The main theory of the Back Game is to have as many men hit and restarted as possible, so that you can get behind your opponent and force him to pass your men again. However, the success of this depends a lot on your opponent's co-operation in hitting your blots as you leave them. An experienced player will try and avoid hitting these blots and make it more difficult for you to add more men to the two men in his Home table.

When Should You Adopt a Back Game?

A Back Game to be effective, must be started early in the game. For instance, if your opponent opened with a throw of (Double Ones) and has occupied four consecutive points while you in return have had a very poor throw. Should he roll another advantageous throw on his next turn your alternative would be to immediately adopt a Back Game.

How the Back Game Is Played

In playing a Back Game, you play just the reverse of what you do in the Running or Block Game.

You must spread as many blots as possible, both in your outer as well as your Home table. Even the 6 point must be broken if necessary to spread blots to force your opponent to hit them by certain throws of the dice.

If you can get four or more men sent back to restart in his Home table, and can manage to occupy three points in his Home table you have a good chance for victory.

The 1 and 2 points and the 4 or 5 points if occupied by your men can bring disaster to your opponent's men as they reach their Home table. Some players prefer to make the 1, 2, and 3 points but my preference is for the 5 or 4 points after the 1 and 2 have been made.

The more men you can contrive to have hit the better, for your possession of these points gives your men stepping stones to hurdle any blockade your opponent has prepared.

Besides aiming to get as many men as possible hit and sent back, another important factor in the Back game is in timing the movement of the pieces outside your opponent's Home table.

It is necessary to slow up the advance of these men as much as possible and to spread a number of them at various points around the board so that when your opponent's men are rehit and travel back you will be in a position to pick them off.

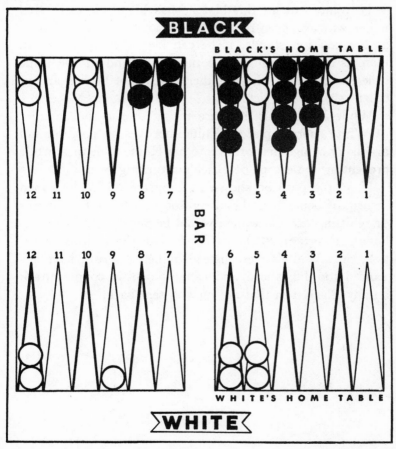

DIAGRAM 28

In Diagram 28 White in playing his Back game has slowed up the progress of his outside pieces and spread them at points along the route where they will have the greatest opportunity of hitting any of Black's men which must retravel around the board.

Black gets a very unfortunate throw of [5] and [6] which compels him to leave a blot on his Bar point.

If White can hit this blot he has his Back game well under way and even though he is about 16 throws behind as the position stands, if he can keep hitting the Black man as it retravels around the board and at the same time succeed in hitting another Black blot he has an excellent chance for victory.

While Black's hit men are trying to run the gauntlet of White's spread pieces, White improves his position and gradually brings his forces into his Home table meanwhile preventing the escape of Black's returning men.

If, in the position shown in Diagram 28 White's men instead of being spread had run too far ahead, his chances of rehitting the Black men would be very slight. The following Diagram 29 shows Black with the identical position, only White's men instead of being spread have advanced too far ahead and can offer little counterattack on any Black men that are hit and sent back.

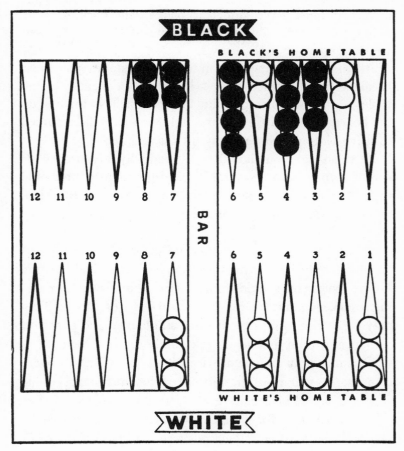

DIAGRAM 29

In this position if Black throws his [6] and [5] and White hits the blot left on Black's Bar point, Black will have little trouble in re-entering his man and passing White's pieces.

To be able to secure this necessary "slowing up" of your

men you must have sufficient pieces sent back to your
opponent's Home table to allow some of them to be used
for playing your high throws.

As the Back Game goes into its last stages you must
break your blockaded points in your opponent's Home
table as this will compel him to play his low throws up
the board and in hitting your single men he will be forced
to leave blots which you may hit on re-entering.

At this stage you should have gradually advanced your
spread men to secure several blocked points in your Home
table. If you can get most of this table closed at this time
and have two of his men on the Bar you have an excellent
chance of winning.

When your opponent has borne most of his men and
you have rehit one of his men and have it locked in your
Home table, you should immediately strip all the remaining Blocked points in his Home table to one man. This
may force him to hit one of these single men and give you
a chance to rehit and send back another of his men.

Ofttimes your opponent's lead is so great that to overcome same you must have two of his men trapped instead of one. By calculating his lead, you can tell whether
this is necessary for you to overtake him. Experienced
players always inspect their positions at regular intervals
during the game and know at any time just how far they
or their opponent are ahead.

By keeping yourself posted on your position you will
know exactly when you have caught up with your opponent and when you find you are several throws ahead you
can abandon your Back Game tactics and race your men
home in the shortest possible moves, using the throws so

that each play will bring a checker from one table to another.

Summing up briefly the strategies of the Back Game are as follows:

1. Leave as many blots as possible in both your inner and outer table to get as many men as possible sent back.

2. Try and secure your opponent's 1 and 2 points, then his 5 or 4 point.

3. Spread your other men so that they can act as sharpshooters to hit any of his men that must retravel around the board.

4. Avoid making blocked points too early in your Home table as blocked points at this stage may delay your opponent which is contrary to your Back Game strategy.

5. As the game reaches the final stages, strip your blocked points in your opponent's Home table to one man on each point to force him to hit these blots. This gives you a good chance of hitting him on re-entering.

6. When you find you have overtaken your opponent and are ahead of him in throws, start your men on the race home.

The Defense Against a Back Game

The best defensive measures to adopt against a Back Game are as follows:

1. Avoid hitting the decoy blots which your opponent is leaving. This will make it difficult for him to add reinforcements to the two men in your Home table.

2. Try and occupy as many points in your Home table as possible to prevent him entering additional men there. If he can only secure your 1 point he will be forced to pile

all his returned men on that one point which will be ineffective if he has not occupied other points in your Home
table. Even if he manages to block your 2 point as well as
the 1, he still will have a difficult road to travel with his
Back Game which to be effective calls for the occupation
of at least three points in your Home table. If he leaves
blots in your Home table in trying to get control of these
vital points, rehit these blots immediately so that he cannot cover same with another man and secure the point.
If he rehits you, it will retard your game which is exactly
what he does not want to do.

For example: Suppose your opponent has switched to
a Back Game and has three men posted on your 1 point
and has two men on the Bar to be re-entered next throw.
He throws a 5 and 2 and places his two men from the
Bar on the 5 and 2 points intending to cover these blots
as soon as possible. If you can strike these blots on your
next throw, you should do so, for it may enable you to
capture and block these points if he fails to rehit your
men.

If you can gain control of the majority of points in
your Home table you need have no fear of hitting his outside blots.

3. If your opponent has succeeded in gaining control
of three points in your Home table your next effort must
be to establish some blocked points in your outer table,
from the 7 to the 12 point. By occupying these points you
can force him to use his high throws by moving his outside men which will result in crowding these men up in
an advanced position in his Home table. In such a situation he would not have his sharpshooters spread to intercept your hit men as they retravel around the board. The

success of his Back Game depends on being able to spread some of his outside men, and if these men have been forced to run far ahead of schedule the backbone of his Back Game is broken.

4. When the Back Game has reached the final stage when your opponent starts to remove his men from your Home table, you should try immediately to secure as many blocked points in your Home table as possible and try to hit some of his men as they race for home.

CHAPTER 5

HOW TO PLAY TO WIN

Backgammon players can be placed in two classes. The first class, those who, having learned the mode of playing the game, depend entirely on the element of chance to win. Their sole standby is the throws of the dice. If luck favors them, they acclaim their victory, but if they lose they excuse their defeat by attributing it to the lucky breaks of their opponent. Such a system of play soon becomes tiresome, especially if your adversary wins game after game, and your espousal of luck loses its conviction.

The other type of Backgammon player plays to win, regardless of the whims of chance. If luck favors him, so much the better, but regardless of good or bad throws of the dice, he puts into his play the fascinating factor of skill.

This player really enjoys the game and in all cases will show a marked superiority over his opponent.

It takes only a few throws of the dice to tell whether or not you are facing a worthy opponent. A player who does not take the best advantage of his opening throws of the dice cannot be expected to play soundly as the game goes on.

Actually, the opening throws play a very important part in the later development and it is necessary for the student to learn exactly how to play these throws to the best advantage.

The following chart shows all the throws of the dice and the proper way to play each to gain the best advantage.

We will start with the Doubles first:

THROWS	BEST PLAY TO BE MADE AT START OF GAME
6 and 6	Move two men from your opponent's 1 point to his 7 or Bar point. Move two men from your opponent's 12 point to your 7 or Bar point. (A very strong throw.) Another strong way of playing this is to move three men to your Bar and one man to your opponent's Bar point.
5 and 5	Two men from your opponent's 12 point to your 3 point. (A very weak throw at start of game.)
4 and 4	Two men from your opponent's 1 point to his 5 point and 2 men from your opponent's 12 point to your 9 point.
3 and 3	There are two excellent ways of playing this throw: Two men from your opponent's 1 to his 4 point, and two men from your 8 to your 5 point—or, many fine players move two men from the opponent's 12 point to your 7 or Bar point.
2 and 2	Two men from your opponent's 1 point to his 5 point.

1 and 1   The best opening throw. Two men from your
          8 to your Bar point, and two men from your 6
          to your 5 point.

The Regular Throws

THROWS   BEST PLAY TO BE MADE AT START OF GAME

6 and 5   One man from your opponent's 1 to his Bar
          point and then to his 12 point.

6 and 4   One man from your opponent's 1 to his Bar
          point and one man from his 1 point to his
          5 point. This is a poor throw, but this is the
          strongest way to play it. The blots may be hit,
          but it is difficult for your opponent to hit them
          and also cover the point, and the risk is well
          worth taking.

          Some players gamble on their luck and play
          a man to their Bar point, but the chances are
          about even of this man being hit.

6 and 3   Two men from your opponent's 1 point to his
          Bar and 4 point.

6 and 2   Two men from opponent's 1 point to his Bar
          and 3 points.

          Some players prefer to play this by moving
          one man to their 5 point; others play a man to
          the Bar point and one to their 11 point, but
          each of these plays are risky.

6 and 1   One man from your opponent's 12 point to
          your Bar point and 1 man from your 8 to your
          7 or Bar point. Another good throw.

5 and 4   One man from your opponent's 1 point to his 5 and one man from his 12 to your 8 point. Some players play this throw by moving two men from the opponent's 12 point, but it is better to try and retreat one of your outposts immediately.

5 and 3   Two men from opponent's 12 point, one to your 8 and one to your 10 point. This gives you builders ready to occupy a Key Point and is stronger than occupying your 3 point.

5 and 2   Two men from your opponent's 12 point, one to your 11 and one to your 8 point.

5 and 1   One man from opponent's 1 point to his Bar point. Many players employ this throw by moving a man from the opponent's 12 to your Bar point, but if your opponent hits this man, he will set you back to such an extent that it is not worth the risk. The same holds true if you play a man to your 8 point and another to your 5 point.

4 and 3   Two men from your opponent's 1 point to his 4 and 5 point. If Black's hits your blots you have a good chance to retaliate by re-hitting his men. Some players play this by moving a man from your opponent's 12 point to their 6 point, but this only piles too many men on one point and gains no advantage.

The Bold School of players move two men from your opponent's 12 point to leave blots on their 9 and 10 points, but the chances are only 3 to 1 against one of these men being hit.

4 and 2   Make your 4 point.

3 and 2 ⎫ Advance your outposts on both these opening
4 and 1 ⎭ throws.

3 and 1   Make your 5 point.

2 and 1   The worst throw on the dice. Your best bet is to move your outpost forward to the 4 point.

The bold player ·in this situation would move one man to his 11 point and one man to his 5 point. The over-cautious player would move a man from the opponent's 12 point to his 10 point.

What Are the Chief Faults of the Beginner?

There are many outstanding faults, which combine to wreck the beginner's game. These I will endeavor to list in the order of their importance.

1. The most important strategy of Backgammon is *to bring your two* furthermost men out of your opponent's Home table. These two men are the weakest members of your forces and you should bring them to safety without any delay. Once you learn this cardinal rule of good play, you will have improved your game many times.

A good Double early in the game will enable you to bring these men out of danger; even a small Double may

give you a chance to move these two men up to your
opponent's 5 point, where you will be in a good position
to advance them further. Also, if you can get these two
men on your opponent's 5 point, it will hinder the progress
of your opponent's pieces, as they arrive at his Home
table. If you advance these two men further to your
opponent's Bar point, it is also a valuable advantage, but
at the start of the game it is wise to hold them on the 5
point in case you decide to switch to a Back Game.

2. *Avoid unnecessary risk.* This comes next in importance to advancing your outposts. The beginner usually
attempts an over bold game, taking all kinds of risks to
make points. This is a very bad fault, for the reckless type
of play generally ends in disaster.

If your opponent wants to takes these chances, you can
profit by his mistakes.

3. Never take up a Blot in your Home table, unless
you can block that point. You must remember that the
men reaching your Home table have theoretically traveled
all around the board, and their value is much greater than
your opponent's two men in your Home table.

If your opponent's men are hit in your Home table, they
are only set back a few points, whereas if your men are
hit in your Home table, they must retravel 19 points to
again reach the point where they were hit.

4. The main objective of the opening game is the need
of securing the advantageous points that will slow up the
advance of your opponent's two men in your Home table.
The most important point to capture first is your 5 point,
then your 7 or Bar point, which starts a powerful blockade on your opponent's two outposts. Many players prefer
the Bar point before the 5 point, but all agree that the Bar

point and the 5 point are the two strongest points to capture. Next in order comes your opponent's 5 point which enables the escape of your two outposts.

5. Never expose a man to being hit unless the risk means a greater risk for your opponent if he takes advantage of it.

6. Another vital tactic the student should learn is shutting out your opponent by closing your Home table. This consists in blocking all the points in your Home table so that if you hit an opponent's blot on some other part of the board, he will be unable to restart the man and must rest idle while you continue to make throw after throw of the dice.

7. The expert Backgammonist always knows at all times exactly how far he is ahead of his opponent or exactly how far his opponent is ahead of him. The best way to reckon the comparative strength or weakness is as follows:

You should first pair any men you and your adversary have on opposite points, then calculate how many points your unpaired men are from the Home table: By making the same calculation with your opponent's unpaired men and comparing the total you can estimate which player is ahead.

A good rule is to survey your position often during the game so you will know just when you must change your tactics or resort to a Back Game.

8. Another important factor to remember is never to crowd your men on your points. Getting a long string of 6 or more men on any point cramps your position and puts a number of your men out of play. Also, avoid playing your men on to the low points in your Home table,

as these men also are out of action and place you at a disadvantage.

9. When compelled to leave a blot, always try and leave it as far away as possible from his advancing men. A blot seven points away from your opponent can only be hit with a combination throw, and the chances of being hit are about 5 to 1 at this distance.

If you are forced to leave a blot within six points of your opponent, leave it as near as possible, one point away being safest.

Also, when leaving a blot, try and choose a point which is more likely to be covered next throw.

10. When the numbers thrown on the dice are not available to make points, let them be used to make preparations for securing points. If your opponent is ` a safe distance away, you can spread these builders so that the following throw will enable you to make another point.

11. Beware of decoy blots left by your opponent, especially if he is a skillful player. Make sure that the blots are forced or attempted at a great risk, and before hitting same, make sure that his Home table is not closed so that if your men are rehit they will be locked out on the Bar.

12. If you have sent one or two of your opponent's men to the bar and have three or more points blocked in your Home table, never fail to spread your oncoming men so that you can make a new point in your Home table or be ready to rehit his men as they re-enter.

13. If your opponent is ahead of you when bearing off, never play up men from your 4 or 3 points while you still have a large number of men on your 6 point. For instance: if you had your 6 point loaded with six checkers and you

got a small throw of a three and a two, it would be best
to move up two men from your 6 point, rather than play
the men up from the lower points. The two men played
forward from the 6 point would leave only four checkers
on that point, and a lucky throw of double sixes would
clear these men from the board and give you a possible
chance of overtaking your opponent. If you had played
up the low throw from the 4 or 5 points, the double sixes
would still leave two men on your 6 point, and the chances
of hitting two more sixes in the next few throws would
be highly improbable.

14. As the game nears a close and the race is neck
and neck, the men must be advanced to the Home table
in the quickest manner possible. The way to do this is to
make plays that will carry a man from one table to another. If you have a man on your opponent's 10 point and
a [3] is thrown, you should move this man across the
table to your 12 point; a play that takes the man into your
outer table. If you had a man on your 12 point and you
throw a [6], you would play this man into your Home
table. By playing your men so that they can go from one
table to another you gain the maximum amount of speed
in bringing them home.

15. Supposing your opponent has locked your two outposts in his Home table on his one Point and has already
brought all his men into his Home table and is bearing off
his men, your only chance of victory is in holding these
men in position in the hopes of his having to leave a blot
as he bears his men and of your hitting same. If he should
open another point in the midst of his men, endeavor
to split up your two men, leaving two blots which form
a greater menace to him, as you still have the opportunity

of hitting him with a favorable throw and you put him in a position where an unfavorable throw on his part may force him to hit one of these blots which then may re-enter and send his man back to start over. If you can establish your two outposts on the 5 point in your opponent's Home table, you are quite safe from any effective block of these two men and your outside men can then be advanced with more effective action.

16. In throwing off, when your adversary still has a man or men in your Home table, try and keep an even number of men upon the points nearest the Bar to avoid an unnecessary blot.

17. In throwing off, when your Home table is closed and your opponent has men on the Bar, it is safest to move men up in your Home table rather than to take men off for the throws. This opens up the High points in your Home table, so that your opponent can enter on these points, which removes the danger of his hitting you on re-entry.

18. In throwing off, after your opponent has passed your men, your aim is to bear off with the quickest possible speed. Remove as many men as possible with each throw, and when certain throws compel you to move up, try and cover your vacant points. A Home board with all points covered is more quickly cleared in bearing.

CHAPTER 6

THE VALUES OF LUCK AND SKILL

While skill plays a very prominent part in sound Backgammon, still the element of Luck is always present. The casts of the dice are always an uncertainty and a player, having a phenomenal succession of lucky throws, might come from behind to win in the home stretch.

While the advanced student should have a knowledge of the possible chances of making certain throws, or the probability of your opponent hitting your man in certain situations, still the player who neglects his general tactics to cater to the laws of probability will soon find that these laws of chance are only based on the averages over a long period of play, and cannot be used as a definite system of Backgammon play.

There are, however, certain occasions in the game wherein a knowledge of mathematical probability can be used to advantage, and especially when you wish to find the safest point to leave an exposed blot.

For instance, suppose you wished to find what were the chances of your opponent throwing a [1] or a [3], compared to the probability of his throwing a [6] or a [7]. This can be figured out as follows: The total number of different throws that can be made with two dice are thirty-six.

A [1] can be thrown on the dice in the following ways: it can be thrown as a Double and it can be thrown in combination with any of the other five numbers on the dice as follows:

$$1 — 1$$

1 — 6	6 — 1
1 — 5	5 — 1
1 — 4	4 — 1
1 — 3	3 — 1
1 — 2	2 — 1

If we add the 10 combination throws of 1 and the double 1, which is counted as one, we have eleven different ways in which a 1 can be thrown.

As there are thirty-six possible throws of the dice, and eleven of them can turn up a 1; therefore, the other 25 throws which will not produce a one make the chances 25 to 11 against a playing throwing a one.

The following computation makes this quite simple:

$$
\begin{aligned}
&36 \text{ possible throws of dice}\\
-\ &11 \text{ chances of making a 1}\\
\hline
=\ &25 \text{ chances against making a one}
\end{aligned}
$$

The chances being 25 to 11 against throwing a 1 (over 2 to 1).

The following table shows the total number of ways that any number on the dice can be thrown:

TABLE NO. 1

Total throws of the Dice = 36

THROWS

1 can be thrown in 11 different ways out of the 36
2 can be thrown in 12 different ways out of the 36
3 can be thrown in 14 different ways out of the 36
4 can be thrown in 15 different ways out of the 36
5 can be thrown in 15 different ways out of the 36
6 can be thrown in 17 different ways out of the 36
7 can be thrown in 6 different ways out of the 36
8 can be thrown in 6 different ways out of the 36
9 can be thrown in 5 different ways out of the 36
10 can be thrown in 3 different ways out of the 36
11 can be thrown in 2 different ways out of the 36
12 can be thrown in 3 different ways out of the 36
15 can be thrown in only 1 way on the dice
16 can be thrown in only 1 way on the dice
18 can be thrown in only 1 way on the dice
20 can be thrown in only 1 way on the dice
24 can be thrown in only 1 way on the dice

Now, having learned the chances of making any number, we can easily know the odds against being hit when we have an exposed blot at any given distance from your opponent's men and he is about to throw.

Table No. 2 gives you the exact and the approximate odds against being hit on any point at any distance from your adversary.

TABLE NO. 2

The odds are 25 to 11 or over 2 to 1 against being hit 1 point away
The odds are 24 to 12 or about 2 to 1 against being hit 2 points away
The odds are 22 to 14 or about 3 to 2 against being hit 3 points away
The odds are 21 to 15 or about 7 to 5 against being hit 4 points away
The odds are 21 to 15 or about 7 to 5 against being hit 5 points away
The odds are 19 to 17 or about even against being hit 6 points away
The odds are 30 to 6 or about 5 to 1 against being hit 7 points away
The odds are 30 to 6 or about 5 to 1 against being hit 8 points away
The odds are 31 to 5 or about 6 to 1 against being hit 9 points away
The odds are 33 to 3 or about 11 to 1 against being hit 10 points away
The odds are 34 to 2 or about 17 to 1 against being hit 11 points away
The odds are 33 to 3 or about 11 to 1 against being hit 12 points away
The odds are 35 to 1 against being hit 15 points away
The odds are 35 to 1 against being hit 16 points away
The odds are 35 to 1 against being hit 18 points away
The odds are 35 to 1 against being hit 20 points away
The odds are 35 to 1 against being hit 24 points away

These are the odds with one blot facing another with all the intervening points being open, but with certain points being blocked the odds change materially. The following examples will explain this:

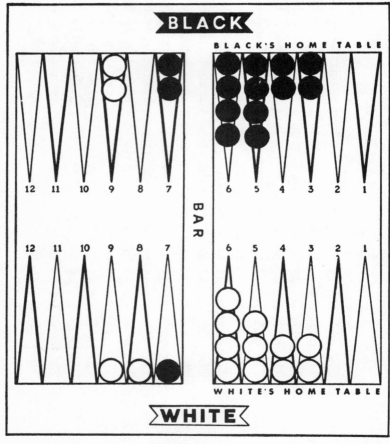

DIAGRAM 30

Black has thrown a [6] and [3] and diagram 30 shows the position. Black has a single man on White's 7 or Bar point, which is open to a direct hit by the two White men immediately in front of him, also by a combination throw of the White men on Black's 9 point. He must bring this man safely home to save his game, and he obviously cannot leave it where it is, exposed to be hit from three different points. He must play the man either for the [6] or the [3].

The question is: shall he play the [6] and land this man on his 12 point, or shall he play the [3] and bring the man to White's 10 point?

If he plays the [6], his man will land three points away from White's two men on Point 9. If he plays the [3], he will land 6 points away.

Which is the safest point to land?

If we refer to Table No. 2, we find that the odds are about even for your opponent throwing a [6], but that the odds are 3 to 2 against his throwing a [3]. Therefore, the Black plays his blot from White's 7 point to his 12 point for the [6] and plays the [3] by advancing a man in his Home Table.

Now, supposing that a similar situation arose wherein some of the intervening points were blocked, the odds would change according to the number of blocked points which cut down the chances of your opponent hitting your man.

The following gives an illustration of this.

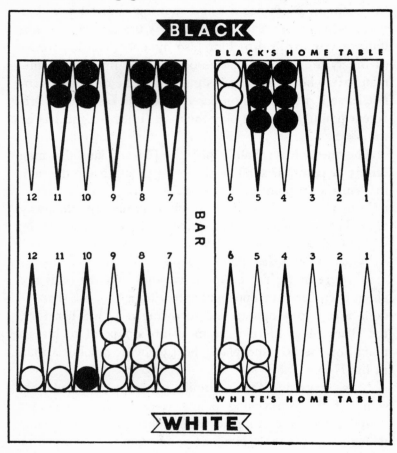

DIAGRAM 31

Here again, it is Black's play and he has thrown a [6] and [3]. As shown in the previous example, he must get his single man on White's 10 out of immediate danger; but shall he play it for the [6] or the [3]?

If he plays the [6], his man will land on his 9 point just 3 points away from White's two men on Black's 6 point.

If this play is made, White must throw a [3] against which the odds, as shown on Table No. 2 are 3 to 2. However, these odds do not apply here, for [Double 1] or [2 and 1] or [1 and 2], throws will not play as Black has these points blocked. White must throw either double threes or a three in combination. In other words, he has only 11 ways out of the 36 possible throws of hitting the man on this point, or over 2 to 1 odds against being hit on this point.

If he plays the man for the [3] and lands on his 12 point, White must throw a [6] to hit him. The regular odds against a six are about even, but here again neither 5—1, 1—5, or 4—2, 2—4 or Double 2 will play and White, only having 12 ways of hitting the man on this point, the odds are about 2 to 1 against.

The final reckoning shows that in this situation, if Black plays his man three points away from White's men on Black's 6 point, White has 11 chances out of 36 of hitting his man, and if he plays it 6 points distant from the White men, White has 12 chances out of the 36 of hitting the man. So, according to the laws of probability, it would be a trifle safer to play the man so that it lands on point 9, where it is three points away from the White men.

While we have gone into these laws of averages at length so that the mathematically inclined player can calculate his laws of averages at critical points, still the student must remember that the dice will often vary greatly from mathematical expectations, and the player who employs alertness and strategy will far excel the player depending on probabilities.

As the game nears its finish and both players have one for more points blocked in their Home table, it becomes difficult for a man that is hit to be re-entered.

Ofttimes, a player at this stage must decide at a glance whether or not he can afford to leave a blot and, if it is hit, what are his chances of re-entering the man in his opponent's Home Table.

The following gives the exact chances of re-entering a man with one or more of the points blocked in your opponent's Home Table.

The student who employs these laws of probability in a general sense will undoubtedly play a much sounder game than the one who takes definite risks merely because the laws of average are slightly in his favor.

For instance, in the table just shown, a player might presume that, as his opponent has three points open in his Home Table, he can run the risk of being hit, as the odds are 3 to 1 that he should be able to re-enter this man.

Placing confidence in such an expectation might be very disappointing, especially where one throw lost might mean the loss of the game.

The player using the table of averages in a more cautious way might deem this risk too great, yet he wouldn't hesitate to be hit when his opponent had four points open with the chances 8 to 1 in his favor.

The cautious player who does not lean too heavily on probability, but who still knows how to calculate his chances and weight them against his risks will prove the finished player.

TABLE NO. 3

The chances are over	2 to 1 against entering a man with only 1 point	open
The chances are	5 to 4 you can enter a man with	2 points open
The chances are	3 to 1 you can enter a man with	3 points open
The chances are	8 to 1 you can enter a man with	4 points open
The chances are	35 to 1 you can enter a man with	5 points open

CHAPTER 7

INSTRUCTIVE EXAMPLES OF PLAY

The following instructive examples illustrate some of the critical situations of the game. The student should try and figure out what play he would make before referring to the answers.

By trying to solve these critical situations on his own initiative he will be able to give himself the same test that would arise if the same positions occurred in actual games. Where he fails to locate the proper play he can refer to the Appended Solution and learn why his judgment was incorrect.

Such exercises give valuable training in the ability to analyze your position at various stages of the game. Also in playing practice games when critical positions arise it would be well to jot down the location of the pieces and if you lose this game you can set up the position later on when you are alone and see if you had a better play.

Problem 1

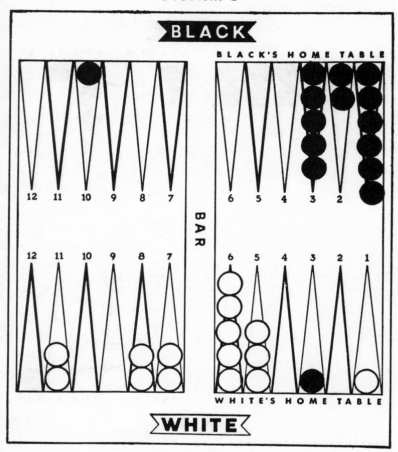

DIAGRAM 32

White Has Thrown a 6 and 2

What play would you make?

Answer—White's best play is to move the man from Point 11 for the entire play. The Black man on 3 must be hit and sent back, even though it means leaving two blots in your Home Table. To break your Bar Point to block the 1 Point would be bad play.

Problem 2

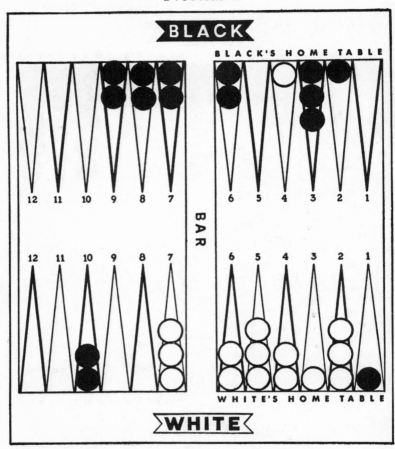

DIAGRAM 33

Black Has Thrown Double Aces

What play would you make?

Answer—The best reply is to play 2 men from your 7 Point to your 5 point. This brings two men into your Home Table by the quickest route and also blocks another point there in case you can later hit a White blot.

Problem 3

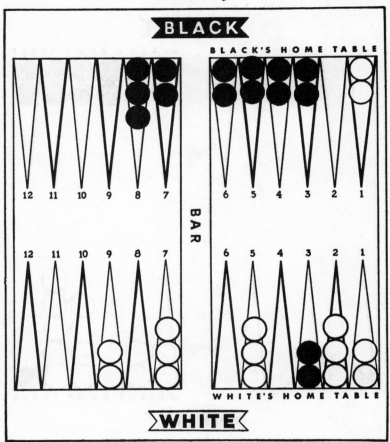

DIAGRAM 34

Black to Play a 4 and 3

What play would you make?

Answer—Play one man from White's 3 point to his 6 to his 10 point. If the blot on the 3 point is hit, Black has a good chance of rehitting this man and securing a Double game. The side prime blockade should not be broken.

Problem 4

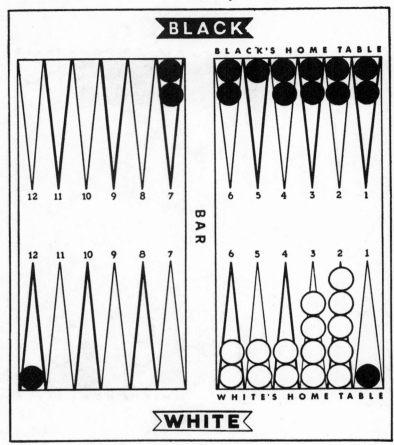

DIAGRAM 35

White to Play a 4 and 1

What play would you make?

Answer—White should play safely by moving two men down from his 6 point, which gives him a certain win. To hit the Black man on 1 Point and send him to the Bar would be an amateurish move and might very easily lose the game.

Problem 5

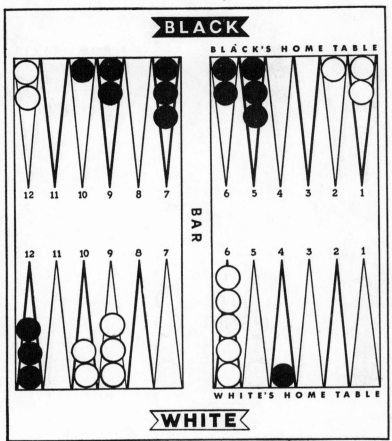

DIAGRAM 36

White to Play a 4 and 2

What play would you make?

Answer—Black is so powerful in this position that White should immediately adopt a Back game. The Blot on 4 should be hit by playing a man from Point 6 for the 2, and then play another man from the 9 to 5 Point for the 4, so that if Black rehit your blots, another White man can be sent to join the three White men already in Black's Home Table. White must expose as many blots as possible.

Problem 6

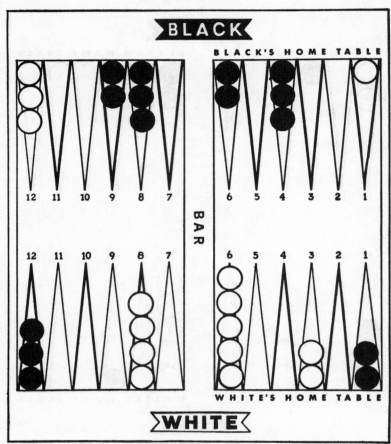

DIAGRAM 37

White to Play Double Sixes

What play would you make?

Answer—White should first play his outpost from Black's
1 Point to his 7 Point. This gives this man a good opportunity for escape. For the other three sixes, move the three
men from Black's 12 to your 7 Point. This starts trouble for
Black's two outposts on your 1 Point.

Problem 7

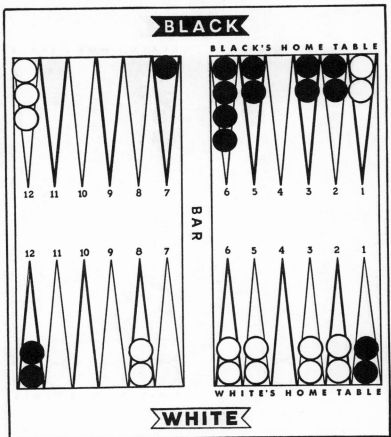

DIAGRAM 38

White to Play a 4 and 2

What play would you make?

Answer—Advance a man from your 8 Point to your 4 Point and continue the same men to your 2 Point. If you moved a man from Black's 12 Point to your 7 Point, your opponent could hit this man with a throw of 6, which he has an even chance of making, but a blot on the 8 Point requires a total of a 6 and 1 or a 3 and 4 to be hit.

Problem 8

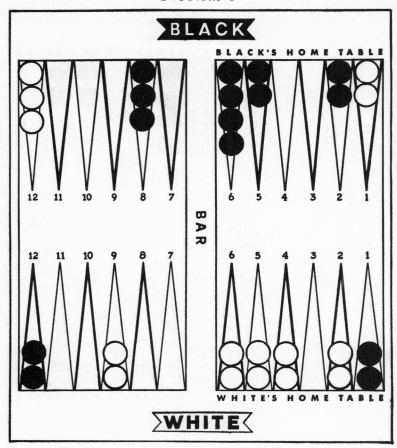

DIAGRAM 39

White to Play a 4 and 1

What play would you make?

Answer—The best play is to move a man from your 9 Point to your 5 to your 4 Point. This gives you an additional builder in your home table and the chance of White hitting the blot left on your 9 Point is about 1 to 17.

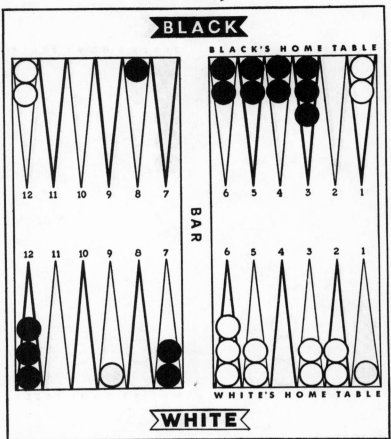

DIAGRAM 40

White to Play a 6 and 5

What play would you make?

Answer—White's best play is to bring one of the outposts from Black's 1 Point to his 12 point. The blot left on the 1 Point may cause Black trouble if he should hit it, as White may rehit him when he restarts. Also, bringing one of the outposts halfway home is a big advantage.

Problem 10

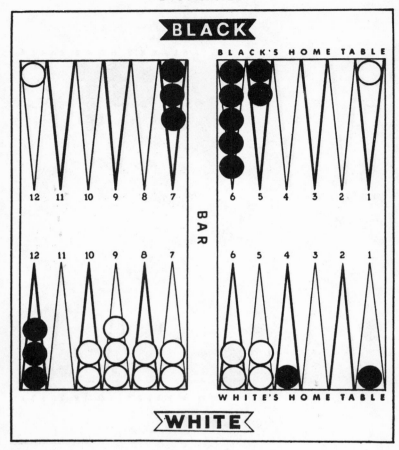

DIAGRAM 41

White to Play a 5 and 4

What play would you make?

Answer—White should play a man from his 9 Point to hit the Black blot on the 4 Point, and then move his man from Black's 12 Point to his 9 Point. If Black rehits the blot on your 4 Point on re-entry, it does not matter because you simply bring the man around the board again while your side prime keeps Black's two men trapped. If Black fails to rehit the man, you may be able to cover him with a man from your 10 or 9 Point on next play.

Problem 11

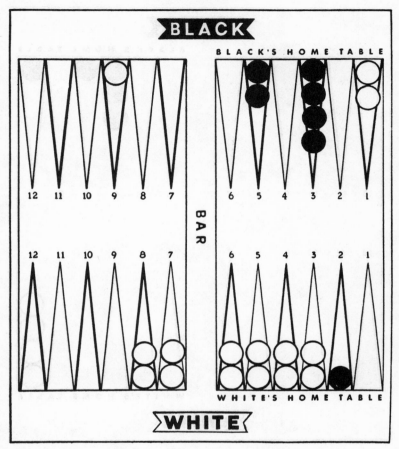

BLACK

BLACK'S HOME TABLE

BAR

WHITE'S HOME TABLE

WHITE

DIAGRAM 42

White to Play a 3 and 5

What play would you make?

Answer—White's best play is to break the two men on his
opponent's 1 point by moving a man to Black's 4 point for the
3 and for the 5 he moves his outside man from Black's 9 point
over to his own 11 point. By opening Black's 1 point, he enables
Black to play a 4 which would force him to hit the White blot
on the 1 point. Black would then have two exposed blots which
White could very likely hit on his next throw. If White can send
back another Black man to be locked in by his Side Prime he
will very likely win the game.

97

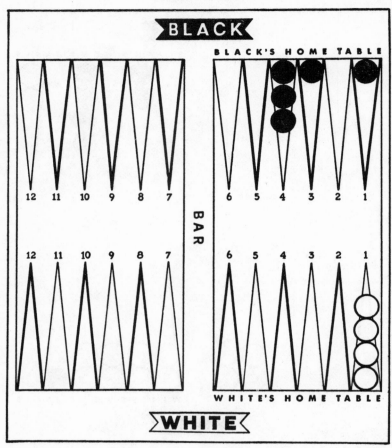

DIAGRAM 43

Black to Play Double Ones

What play would you make?

Answer—Black must play one man off the 1 point and play three men down from the 4th point to the 3 point.

White is bound to go out in two throws and Black's only chance for a win is in hitting a high double. If he throws off the men on the 1 and 3 points then the only doubles that will win for him are double fours, fives or sixes. By playing the three men down from his 4 point then double threes would also win.

CHAPTER 8

DOUBLING AND CHOUETTE

The introduction of "Doubling" is a modern addition to the game and simply means that the players have the option of Doubling the stakes during the progress of the game.

A player finding that the game has turned in his favor can, after his opponent has completed his throw, double the initial stake. If the opponent refuses the Doubling of the stakes, he forfeits the game and the original stake. Should he decide that he still has chances of winning, he can accept the Double and the game goes on.

However, the player who has offered the first double cannot double the stakes again. The privilege of making another Double rests with his opponent, who may double the stakes again if he wishes it. If he does, the first player must accept or resign and pay the Double stakes, or accept with the game proceeding with the stakes being four times the original amount.

There is no limit to the number of doubles, although the option of offering it changes from one player to another each time. So that one player cannot redouble consecutively.

This innovation of Doubling has appealed to a great class of people who like action with their games, and also it has emphasized the vital importance of skill at the game.

A player who can correctly estimate his position will know when to accept and when to refuse a Double, for if a game is hopeless, it is far better to forfeit the original stakes than to have it Doubled and still play on to inevitable defeat.

A certain amount of psychology also enters Backgammon with the advent of Doubling, for a clever player can take advantage of an opponent who looks upon a Double as a challenge to his courage and refuses to forfeit a hopeless game.

Also, a shrewd player pitted against an over cautious or timid opponent will take advantage of a few good throws to offer a bluff Double to scare him out of the game when he still has a reasonable chance of victory.

It is certain that judgment and the ability to appraise your game are qualities very vital to play a Doubling game. If you are an inexperienced player, it would be most sensible to refrain from a Doubling game, for a skilful adversary would have you at a great disadvantage.

Generally, more is lost by the unsound acceptance of a well timed Double. Once you have achieved the ability of being able to calculate your position any time in the game, you will know when to accept or resign when your opponent offers a Double. Also, you will know when it is your own advantage to Double. The best time to Double is early in the game if you find you have an unquestionably strong position.

When both players are bearing off and you find you are several throws ahead, you can eliminate any possible long shots your opponent might get by Doubling the stakes. The opponent rather than gamble on the long odds of winning will almost certainly resign. If his courage is better than his wisdom and he decides to accept the Double, then you still have everything in your favor with the winning stakes Doubled. In throwing off the men, you can generally calculate throwing off two men to a throw.

If it is your throw, and you have already thrown off 7 men to your opponent's 6, you can figure you are a throw and a half ahead, for your present throw will presumably remove two men more. In estimating the throws, the general basis is to consider that each throw removes two men. Obviously a throw of doublets by either player gains an extra throw.

Experience in actual play is the best teacher as to when and when not to Double, but in the meantime, caution is the best safeguard against rash and costly Doubling.

Chouette

Chouette is simply a new innovation which allows interested bystanders to wager on the outcome of the game. They only take turns in the playing after the active player is defeated and turns over his seat to one of these co-players.

Assuming you have a Backgammon group, each player throws one dice and the highest thrower is entitled to play "in the box."

The next highest thrower becomes the opponent who plays against the man in the box, and the others present simply back the play of this opponent with their stake.

If the player "in the box" wins, he collects from his opponent and also collects from each of the others on the sidelines. If the player in the box loses, he must pay his opponent in the game, also the co-players who have also wagered their stakes.

When the player in the "Box" is defeated, he retires to the sidelines, the winning opponent taking the "box" and another player from the group sitting in to play against him.

The game itself is played as usual, Doubles, and Re-doubles and Gammons increasing the stakes in the customary manner.

The player competing against the man in the "Box" is allowed to confer with the players that are allied with him, but if any discussion arises, the player himself has the final decision as to what play he wishes to make.

If the player against the "Box" wishes to Double and his partners do not wish to take the risk, the partners must forfeit their stakes to the player, who then continues the game on his own responsibility, accepting all financial liabilities both his own and his partners who have retired from participation.

CHAPTER 9

RULES OF BACKGAMMON

1. The Backgammon board must be set up in the standard way with the Home Tables either to the right or left, the selection being decided by the player winning the opening throw.

2. The choice of the men, also the first play goes to the player making the highest opening throw at the start of the game. The opening throw is made with each player throwing a single die, the winner using the numbers on both his own and his opponent's die for his first play. After the first play, each player uses both dice.

3. If, after the game has started, it is found that some of the men have been set up in the wrong position, the game must be started over again.

4. To constitute a proper throw, the dice must be shaken in the dice box and cast in the players right hand table.

5. In being rolled on the board, the dice must rest flat on the surface. If they do not rest in this position or are tilted, or thrown out of the Right hand table, the throw is adjudged faulty and must be made over again.

6. If one or both dice are touched by either player while rolling or before the player has called the numbers showing, the throw must be made again.

7. Once a player has completed a play to any given point and removed his hand from the piece, he cannot change his play.

8. If an incorrect play is made, the opponent can demand that the error be corrected, provided he points out the mistake before he has made his own throw. If same is discovered later, it can only be adjusted by mutual consent.

9. The whole of the two numbers thrown on the dice must be played if possible, but if only one can be played, the highest number must be played.

10. A player is not allowed to make his throw of the dice until his opponent's play has been completed.

11. A *single game* is won by the first player who throws off all his men.

12. A *Double game* is known as a *"Gammon"* and is won by the player who has thrown off all his men before his opponent has removed a man.

13. A *Triple Game* is known as a *"Backgammon"* and is won by the player who succeeds in throwing off all his men before his opponent has thrown off a man, and still has men in the winner's Home Table or upon the Bar.

14. In playing "Doubles," the players must agree on whether the optional and automatic Double will be adopted.

(a) If the automatic Double is adopted, when the opening throw of one die is the same, the stakes are automatically doubled and the players throw again. If tied again, the stakes are again doubled and the process goes on unless the players have agreed upon a limit to these opening Doubles.

(b) The optional double allows either player to offer the first Doubling of the original stakes. Thereafter, the right to Double the stakes always rests with the player who has accepted the last Double. A Double can be offered only when it is the player's turn to play and before he has cast his throw.

CHAPTER 10

ACEY-DEUCEY

A game very popular with the men of the U. S. Navy is known as Acey-Deucey.

It is a variation of Backgammon, played on the same board—only the pieces are not set up on the board at the start of the game, but are played onto the board. Each player throws the two dice at the start of the game, and the highest wins, and then rethrows for his first move.

The player enters his men in the left hand table on his side of the board, and his opponent's men are entered directly opposite. The plays are made according to the throws of the dice, as in regular Backgammon, the men moving in opposite directions around the board to the table where his opponent's men were started.

The men can be advanced as soon as they are entered on the board, but a player cannot start bearing his men until the entire number have been entered and advanced to his Home Table.

The other rules of regular Backgammon apply as to Blocked Points, Hits, and re-entered men.

If Doublets are thrown, double the number of moves may be made, plus the double on the bottom side of the dice. Also Doublets entitles the player to another throw of the dice. If Doublets are thrown again, the same procedure is followed, both sides of the dice are played and an extra throw allowed.

Four men can be entered for a Double throw on the corresponding Point, or part of the men can be entered and the rest of the throw played around the board.

The game derived its name from the fact that every time an Ace or Deuce is thrown, the player, after making his move, is entitled to select and play any double and is allowed another extra throw of the dice.

In bearing off, the men can only be thrown off from the point that corresponds with the numbers thrown, but a man cannot be removed from the next highest point, as in regular Backgammon. In a case where a 6 is thrown and there is no man on that point, but a man on the 5, the player cannot remove the man on the 5 point but loses his play.

The scoring is usually done on the basis of a Single Game.

A Few Golden Rules to Remember

1. Take your time and study each play. Also, do not try and hurry your opponent.

2. Pay attention to your own game and try and not criticize or make comments on your opponent's plays.

3. Do not rattle the dice when it is not your turn to play. Also, do not drum on the table, whistle or otherwise annoy your opponent.

4. Lose with good grace and sportsmanship, and remember that the main purpose of the game is entertainment.

5. Do not make your moves with such rapidity that your opponent cannot follow the plays.

6. Never touch a piece until you are certain you are going to play it.

7. Don't take too great risks during the game, for a sound game is generally a cautious one.

8. Try and play with better players, as this is one of the best means of improving your game.

INDEX

A CATALOGUE OF SELECTED DOVER BOOKS
IN ALL FIELDS OF INTEREST

A CATALOGUE OF SELECTED DOVER BOOKS
IN ALL FIELDS OF INTEREST

AMERICA'S OLD MASTERS, James T. Flexner. Four men emerged unexpectedly from provincial 18th century America to leadership in European art: Benjamin West, J. S. Copley, C. R. Peale, Gilbert Stuart. Brilliant coverage of lives and contributions. Revised, 1967 edition. 69 plates. 365pp. of text.
21806-6 Paperbound $3.00

FIRST FLOWERS OF OUR WILDERNESS: AMERICAN PAINTING, THE COLONIAL PERIOD, James T. Flexner. Painters, and regional painting traditions from earliest Colonial times up to the emergence of Copley, West and Peale Sr., Foster, Gustavus Hesselius, Feke, John Smibert and many anonymous painters in the primitive manner. Engaging presentation, with 162 illustrations. xxii + 368pp.
22180-6 Paperbound $3.50

THE LIGHT OF DISTANT SKIES: AMERICAN PAINTING, 1760-1835, James T. Flexner. The great generation of early American painters goes to Europe to learn and to teach: West, Copley, Gilbert Stuart and others. Allston, Trumbull, Morse; also contemporary American painters—primitives, derivatives, academics—who remained in America. 102 illustrations. xiii + 306pp.
22179-2 Paperbound $3.00

A HISTORY OF THE RISE AND PROGRESS OF THE ARTS OF DESIGN IN THE UNITED STATES, William Dunlap. Much the richest mine of information on early American painters, sculptors, architects, engravers, miniaturists, etc. The only source of information for scores of artists, the major primary source for many others. Unabridged reprint of rare original 1834 edition, with new introduction by James T. Flexner, and 394 new illustrations. Edited by Rita Weiss. 6⅝ x 9⅝.
21695-0, 21696-9, 21697-7 Three volumes, Paperbound $13.50

EPOCHS OF CHINESE AND JAPANESE ART, Ernest F. Fenollosa. From primitive Chinese art to the 20th century, thorough history, explanation of every important art period and form, including Japanese woodcuts; main stress on China and Japan, but Tibet, Korea also included. Still unexcelled for its detailed, rich coverage of cultural background, aesthetic elements, diffusion studies, particularly of the historical period. 2nd, 1913 edition. 242 illustrations. lii + 439pp. of text.
20364-6, 20365-4 Two volumes, Paperbound $6.00

THE GENTLE ART OF MAKING ENEMIES, James A. M. Whistler. Greatest wit of his day deflates Oscar Wilde, Ruskin, Swinburne; strikes back at inane critics, exhibitions, art journalism; aesthetics of impressionist revolution in most striking form. Highly readable classic by great painter. Reproduction of edition designed by Whistler. Introduction by Alfred Werner. xxxvi + 334pp.
21875-9 Paperbound $2.50

ADVENTURES OF AN AFRICAN SLAVER, Theodore Canot. Edited by Brantz Mayer. A detailed portrayal of slavery and the slave trade, 1820-1840. Canot, an established trader along the African coast, describes the slave economy of the African kingdoms, the treatment of captured negroes, the extensive journeys in the interior to gather slaves, slave revolts and their suppression, harems, bribes, and much more. Full and unabridged republication of 1854 edition. Introduction by Malcom Cowley. 16 illustrations. xvii + 448pp. 22456-2 Paperbound $3.50

MY BONDAGE AND MY FREEDOM, Frederick Douglass. Born and brought up in slavery, Douglass witnessed its horrors and experienced its cruelties, but went on to become one of the most outspoken forces in the American anti-slavery movement. Considered the best of his autobiographies, this book graphically describes the in-human treatment of slaves, its effects on slave owners and slave families, and how Douglass's determination led him to a new life. Unaltered reprint of 1st (1855) edition. xxxii + 464pp. 22457-0 Paperbound $2.50

THE INDIANS' BOOK, recorded and edited by Natalie Curtis. Lore, music, narratives, dozens of drawings by Indians themselves from an authoritative and important survey of native culture among Plains, Southwestern, Lake and Pueblo Indians. Standard work in popular ethnomusicology. 149 songs in full notation. 23 draw-ings, 23 photos. xxxi + 584pp. 6⅝ x 9⅜. 21939-9 Paperbound $4.50

DICTIONARY OF AMERICAN PORTRAITS, edited by Hayward and Blanche Cirker. 4024 portraits of 4000 most important Americans, colonial days to 1905 (with a few important categories, like Presidents, to present). Pioneers, explorers, colonial figures, U. S. officials, politicians, writers, military and naval men, scientists, inven-tors, manufacturers, jurists, actors, historians, educators, notorious figures, Indian chiefs, etc. All authentic contemporary likenesses. The only work of its kind in existence; supplements all biographical sources for libraries. Indispensable to any-one working with American history. 8,000-item classified index, finding lists, other aids. xiv + 756pp. 9¼ x 12¾. 21823-6 Clothbound $30.00

TRITTON'S GUIDE TO BETTER WINE AND BEER MAKING FOR BEGINNERS, S. M. Tritton. All you need to know to make family-sized quantities of over 100 types of grape, fruit, herb and vegetable wines; as well as beers, mead, cider, etc. Com-plete recipes, advice as to equipment, procedures such as fermenting, bottling, and storing wines. Recipes given in British, U. S., and metric measures. Accompanying booklet lists sources in U. S. A. where ingredients may be bought, and additional information. 11 illustrations. 157pp. 5⅝ x 8⅛. (USO) 22090-7 Clothbound $3.50

GARDENING WITH HERBS FOR FLAVOR AND FRAGRANCE, Helen M. Fox. How to grow herbs in your own garden, how to use them in your cooking (over 55 recipes included), legends and myths associated with each species, uses in medicine, per-fumes, etc.—these are elements of one of the few books written especially for Amer-ican herb fanciers. Guides you step-by-step from soil preparation to harvesting and storage for each type of herb. 12 drawings by Louise Mansfield. xiv + 334pp. 22540-2 Paperbound $2.50

CATALOGUE OF DOVER BOOKS

INCIDENTS OF TRAVEL IN YUCATAN, John L. Stephens. Classic (1843) exploration of jungles of Yucatan, looking for evidences of Maya civilization. Stephens found many ruins; comments on travel adventures, Mexican and Indian culture. 127 striking illustrations by F. Catherwood. Total of 669 pp.
20926-1, 20927-X Two volumes, Paperbound $5.00

INCIDENTS OF TRAVEL IN CENTRAL AMERICA, CHIAPAS, AND YUCATAN, John L. Stephens. An exciting travel journal and an important classic of archeology. Narrative relates his almost single-handed discovery of the Mayan culture, and exploration of the ruined cities of Copan, Palenque, Utatlan and others; the monuments they dug from the earth, the temples buried in the jungle, the customs of poverty-stricken Indians living a stone's throw from the ruined palaces. 115 drawings by F. Catherwood. Portrait of Stephens. xii + 812pp.
22404-X, 22405-8 Two volumes, Paperbound $6.00

A NEW VOYAGE ROUND THE WORLD, William Dampier. Late 17-century naturalist joined the pirates of the Spanish Main to gather information; remarkably vivid account of buccaneers, pirates; detailed, accurate account of botany, zoology, ethnography of lands visited. Probably the most important early English voyage, enormous implications for British exploration, trade, colonial policy. Also most interesting reading. Argonaut edition, introduction by Sir Albert Gray. New introduction by Percy Adams. 6 plates, 7 illustrations. xlvii + 376pp. 6½ x 9¼.
21900-3 Paperbound $3.00

INTERNATIONAL AIRLINE PHRASE BOOK IN SIX LANGUAGES, Joseph W. Bátor. Important phrases and sentences in English paralleled with French, German, Portuguese, Italian, Spanish equivalents, covering all possible airport-travel situations; created for airline personnel as well as tourist by Language Chief, Pan American Airlines. xiv + 204pp.
22017-6 Paperbound $2.00

STAGE COACH AND TAVERN DAYS, Alice Morse Earle. Detailed, lively account of the early days of taverns; their uses and importance in the social, political and military life; furnishings and decorations; locations; food and drink; tavern signs, etc. Second half covers every aspect of early travel; the roads, coaches, drivers, etc. Nostalgic, charming, packed with fascinating material. 157 illustrations, mostly photographs. xiv + 449pp.
22518-6 Paperbound $4.00

NORSE DISCOVERIES AND EXPLORATIONS IN NORTH AMERICA, Hjalmar R. Holand. The perplexing Kensington Stone, found in Minnesota at the end of the 19th century. Is it a record of a Scandinavian expedition to North America in the 14th century? Or is it one of the most successful hoaxes in history. A scientific detective investigation. Formerly *Westward from Vinland*. 31 photographs, 17 figures. x + 354pp.
22014-1 Paperbound $2.75

A BOOK OF OLD MAPS, compiled and edited by Emerson D. Fite and Archibald Freeman. 74 old maps offer an unusual survey of the discovery, settlement and growth of America down to the close of the Revolutionary war: maps showing Norse settlements in Greenland, the explorations of Columbus, Verrazano, Cabot, Champlain, Joliet, Drake, Hudson, etc., campaigns of Revolutionary war battles, and much more. Each map is accompanied by a brief historical essay. xvi + 299pp. 11 x 13¾.
22084-2 Paperbound $6.00

MATHEMATICAL PUZZLES FOR BEGINNERS AND ENTHUSIASTS, Geoffrey Mott-Smith. 189 puzzles from easy to difficult—involving arithmetic, logic, algebra, properties of digits, probability, etc.—for enjoyment and mental stimulus. Explanation of mathematical principles behind the puzzles. 135 illustrations. viii + 248pp.
20198-8 Paperbound $1.75

PAPER FOLDING FOR BEGINNERS, William D. Murray and Francis J. Rigney. Easiest book on the market, clearest instructions on making interesting, beautiful origami. Sail boats, cups, roosters, frogs that move legs, bonbon boxes, standing birds, etc. 40 projects; more than 275 diagrams and photographs. 94pp.
20713-7 Paperbound $1.00

TRICKS AND GAMES ON THE POOL TABLE, Fred Herrmann. 79 tricks and games— some solitaires, some for two or more players, some competitive games—to entertain you between formal games. Mystifying shots and throws, unusual caroms, tricks involving such props as cork, coins, a hat, etc. Formerly *Fun on the Pool Table*. 77 figures. 95pp.
21814-7 Paperbound $1.00

HAND SHADOWS TO BE THROWN UPON THE WALL: A SERIES OF NOVEL AND AMUSING FIGURES FORMED BY THE HAND, Henry Bursill. Delightful picturebook from great-grandfather's day shows how to make 18 different hand shadows: a bird that flies, duck that quacks, dog that wags his tail, camel, goose, deer, boy, turtle, etc. Only book of its sort. vi + 33pp. 6½ x 9¼.   21779-5 Paperbound $1.00

WHITTLING AND WOODCARVING, E. J. Tangerman. 18th printing of best book on market. "If you can cut a potato you can carve" toys and puzzles, chains, chessmen, caricatures, masks, frames, woodcut blocks, surface patterns, much more. Information on tools, woods, techniques. Also goes into serious wood sculpture from Middle Ages to present, East and West. 464 photos, figures. x + 293pp.
20965-2 Paperbound $2.00

HISTORY OF PHILOSOPHY, Julián Marias. Possibly the clearest, most easily followed, best planned, most useful one-volume history of philosophy on the market; neither skimpy nor overfull. Full details on system of every major philosopher and dozens of less important thinkers from pre-Socratics up to Existentialism and later. Strong on many European figures usually omitted. Has gone through dozens of editions in Europe. 1966 edition, translated by Stanley Appelbaum and Clarence Strowbridge. xviii + 505pp.   21739-6 Paperbound $3.00

YOGA: A SCIENTIFIC EVALUATION, Kovoor T. Behanan. Scientific but non-technical study of physiological results of yoga exercises; done under auspices of Yale U. Relations to Indian thought, to psychoanalysis, etc. 16 photos. xxiii + 270pp.
20505-3 Paperbound $2.50

Prices subject to change without notice.
Available at your book dealer or write for free catalogue to Dept. GI, Dover Publications, Inc., 180 Varick St., N. Y., N. Y. 10014. Dover publishes more than 150 books each year on science, elementary and advanced mathematics, biology, music, art, literary history, social sciences and other areas.